GW00729887

LANDBRIDGE

[life in fragments]

LANDBRIDGE

[life in fragments]

Y-DANG TROEUNG

ALLEN LANE
an imprint of
PENGUIN BOOKS

ALLEN LANE

UK | USA | Canada | Ireland | Australia
India | New Zealand | South Africa

Allen Lane is part of the Penguin Random House group of companies
whose addresses can be found at global.penguinrandomhouse.com.

First published in Canada by Alchemy, a division of
Penguin Random House Canada 2023
First published in Great Britain by Allen Lane 2023

001

Copyright © Y-Dang Troeung, 2023

The moral right of the author has been asserted

Printed and bound in Great Britain by Clays Ltd, Elcograf S.p.A.

Image credits: (watercolour) WONG FOK LOY /
Getty Images; (texture) svetlanais/ Adobe Stock

The authorized representative in the EEA is Penguin Random House Ireland,
Morrison Chambers, 32 Nassau Street, Dublin D02 YH68

A CIP catalogue record for this book is available from the British Library

ISBN: 978-0-241-64800-1

www.greenpenguin.co.uk

MIX
Paper | Supporting
responsible forestry
FSC® C018179

Penguin Random House is committed to a
sustainable future for our business, our readers
and our planet. This book is made from Forest
Stewardship Council® certified paper.

This book is dedicated to my family: Yok Troeung, Heung Troeung, Meng Troeung, Pheng Troeung, Sophia Troeung, Mary Tsoi, Christopher Patterson, and Kai Basilio Troeung.

And to all Cambodian people, with love.

[preface]

The intensity of these accounts, the imprint they leave on me, does not lessen with each telling.

A quarter of Cambodia's population died during the genocide; the remaining three-quarters were physically and mentally debilitated.

US bombings, the Khmer Rouge genocide, toxic and carcinogenic exposure, incarceration, urban and rural divestment, deportation.

In this book, theory, fiction, and autobiography blur through allusive fragments. These fragments—a perforated language of cracks and breaks—seek to knit together, however imperfectly, the lifeworlds that inspire me to write here, on this page.

I seek the regenerative possibilities of speaking for myself as a Cambodian refugee. I do not seek to speak for all refugees or all Cambodians, or even some of them, including my family members, whose stories I have reproduced here (as filtered through my own recollections) with their consent and collaborative curation.

My public image as a refugee child rescued from Cambodia has been made and remade frequently throughout my life in ways that have been largely out of my control.

I am sensitive to the vital issue of voice and appropriation as it relates to life stories and testimonials. Having your story told for you can be painful and wounding, especially when you do not see yourself in someone else's carefully crafted portrait.

For my mother and father, the ruination of wartime is forever etched in their memory, and it remains alive with us, we who carry these histories forward. Dwelling in their memories, I write now of myself, in dialogue with the lifeworlds of my community.

land bridge

A connection between two land masses, especially continents, that allows the migration of plants and animals from one land mass to the other.

Michael Allaby, *A Dictionary of Zoology*

My mother holding me at nine months old with cousins (person second-to-left unknown) at Khao-I-Dang (KID) Holding Center, Thailand, September 1, 1980. Courtesy of the Troeung family. Photo by unknown.

[portrait]

The image opposite was taken in the refugee camp where I was born. In the background, the mountains of Khao-I-Dang loom, forming a picturesque backdrop for six refugees (my mother, me, an unknown girl, and three members of my extended family). A story of pain subtends and saturates this image—death, illness, disappearance, starvation, forced marriage, child loss, and so much more.

As I look upon this image now, I do not see a portrait of suffering. I see a serendipitous, reconstituted family. I see a mother's fleeting instance of joy born out of a chance encounter with another Cambodian refugee in the camp looking to make a few extra dollars with his Polaroid camera.

What mother would not want a photo—at least one photo— of her new baby in that fragile first year of her life?

[transport]

My mother tells me the story of my birth. It is 1979 at the Thai-Cambodian border. Every day, a Red Cross bus arrives in the morning to transport people across the border, into Thailand. After four years of deprivation under the Khmer Rouge, the refugees hope to reach Khao-I-Dang, a camp run by the United Nations and rumoured to be safe. We are at a border camp called Chumrum Thmei that is vulnerable to attacks. The genocide is over, but the war rages on among different militia groups.

When the bus arrives one particular morning, my parents are determined to get on it. They sense an imminent danger and know the time has come to pick up and leave, yet again. In the crowd of refugees pushing forward, they jostle in front of the bus, hoping to be selected. Knowing the sick and the pregnant are given priority, my mother shows her eight-months-pregnant belly to the Red Cross workers and manages to secure a spot for our family. They board the bus and leave Cambodia for the last time.

After a sixteen-hour journey, my family arrives at Khao-I-Dang Holding Center, a sprawling camp inhabited by more than 130,000 people. Soon after they get off the bus, my parents hear

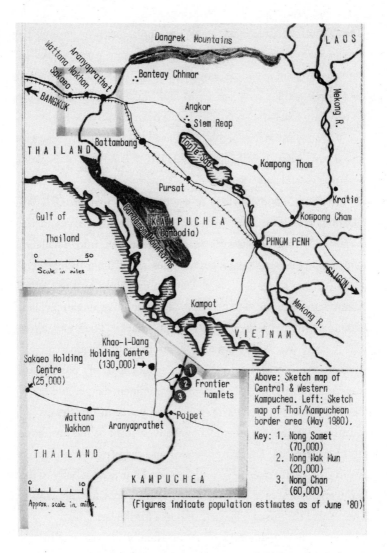

*Khao-I-Dang Holding Center on a hand-drawn map, made
by relief worker Colin Grafton, 1980. Courtesy of the artist.*

the news about an attack. The night before, Khmer Rouge soldiers had arrived at the Chumrum Thmei border camp on the Cambodian side, ransacking and burning it down to nothing but rubble and ash. Everyone my family knew at the camp was killed, captured, or subjected to worse horrors. It shamed my parents to marvel at their luck yet again. But they also felt that finally, in reaching Khao-I-Dang, they had crossed into a new life.

When my mother tells this story, she likes to emphasize the part about my presence in her womb. *I think it is because of Y-Dang, because I was pregnant with her. That's why we got lucky.*

In Khmer, giving birth is referred to as *chlong tonle* (ឆ្លងទន្លេ) meaning *to cross a river*.

My mother gives birth to me in Khao-I-Dang (เขาอีไล) about one month after our arrival there. In Thai, *khao* (เขา) means mountain. *I-Dang* (อีไล) is the name of the mountain near the camp. The camp takes the name of the mountain. My name, Y-Dang Troeung, ទ្រឿងអ៊ីដាង, Mom and Dad always remind me, carries the memory of our survival through multiple crossings.

[currency]

On April 17, 1975, my mother and father, along with my two brothers, walk outside the front door of their home in Kampong Thom, Cambodia, their arms full of food and gifts to welcome the Khmer Rouge soldiers who march into the city. They feel relieved to go back outside. The war, the bombings, and the rockets have come to an end. My mother, a slight woman, resourceful and beautiful, and my father, a gentle rebel, huddle their young boys close to them.

The Khmer Rouge tell people to pack up their belongings and prepare to leave their homes for three days. My mother and father's expressions turn to worry, then fear, then dread. The Khmer Rouge announce warnings that the Americans plan to bomb again. All those in possession of arms must lay them down in the town square. My mother goes to dig up a jar of *riel*, Cambodian currency she had buried in preparation for this day; but as she does so, the Khmer Rouge suddenly announce that money, as well as books, art, and religion, are abolished in the new Democratic Kampuchea.

Banks are blown up. Libraries, cinemas, and temples are destroyed. My parents watch as soldiers point their guns at people who refuse to vacate their homes. They watch as strangers, friends, and neighbours are rounded up and taken away.

Decades later, my mother and father tell me that it was a trap. They were not allowed to return to their homes in three days. Instead, they walked. They walked for days and nights into the jungle, into the new Cambodia, Year Zero. They crossed into new lives that would be shattered and remade again and again over the next four decades.

[hunger]

It is 1979, the last days of what Cambodian people often call *samay a-Pot*, or in English, *Pol Pot time*. The Khmer Rouge have been ousted by the Vietnamese army and my parents find themselves back in their hometown of Kampong Thom. They have survived. But shame washes over them when they think of those who did not. *One more year and we all would have been dead*. They are not living in their old home from before the war, but in a different abandoned building. *We just stayed wherever we could, in those destroyed homes*. The Khmer Rouge are no longer in control, but the march of war fumes ever forward. *We didn't have enough of anything. Not enough. Not enough water. No money. Nothing*.

One day, my brother begs for more food and my mother goes to the market to buy a hen. Watching her children live on the brink of starvation for four years has led her to a place beyond sanity, beyond madness, to something more excruciating, more feral. No mother should have to live with the image of her children in such pain.

My mother sets out to get what my brother needs. She carries, pinned in her pocket, a carefully concealed bag of jewellery, valuables and heirlooms she managed to hide throughout Pol Pot time by burying it in the ground. The only hen still available at the market looks demonic, possessed by the devil. After my mother pays for it, she realizes that someone has loosened the pin in her jacket pocket. The bag of jewellery is gone.

With this loss, my mother feels as if something inside her has finally come undone. Inside the bag were two diamond bracelets given to her by her beloved mother, whose body was never found, whose spirit now wanders restlessly. These items are all my mother had left to mourn her mother. And without the jewellery, she has nothing to trade for food.

My mother wonders now how her children will survive. *I went so crazy during this time.* She cries uncontrollably. A friend tries to comfort her. He says to her in Fujian, my mother's father's native language, 你哭有什么样? *My child, what is the use of crying now?*

My mother starts to feel ill as the days pass. She vomits frequently and then one day she realizes that she is pregnant. It has been eight years since her last pregnancy. She cannot believe she is bringing a child into *this* world.

Dearest Kai *(Kai-bear, puppy finger, nugget baby, nugs)*,

You have brought your father and me so much joy in your first year of life. When you came out of my womb at Pamela Youde Eastern Hospital in Hong Kong on August 30, 2017 at 1 a.m., you were crying and squealing like a little baby dragon. We instantly fell in love with you. You had such a big head and little body (as you still do!) and looked up at us with your big beautiful brown eyes. You looked so much like your father with your pretty eyelashes.

When we brought you home to our flat in Sai Wan Ho, we had so many, many, many nights where you kept us awake until we all watched the sun come up, but every moment was worth it! In your first year, your Tita Anne helped us take very good care of you in Hong Kong. She fed you and bathed you and loved you. Since our own parents could not be here, she taught us to be the best parents we could be, and we owe her so much.

As a baby of just one month, you developed a fascination with going for long walks on the harbour and sometimes your dad and I would take you out five or six times a day! We think you are destined to be an adventurer and explorer. We took you all over Hong Kong: Stanley Beach, Victoria Park, Shek O, Wan Chai,

Chai Wan, and especially Quarry Bay. My long walks with you, my beloved Kai, saved me this year when things felt hopeless. After a difficult pregnancy and birth, I could only spend ten weeks with you before going back to work, and then having to find a new job back in Canada. But after around five months, you started laughing in such a hilarious way. Your laugh and your smile melt our hearts and bring us joy no matter the hardships we face.

When we flew from Hong Kong to Hualien, Taiwan, for our first family vacation, we were terrified about what could happen, but you were a dream to travel with! You did not cry once on the plane or during the entire trip. As long as we had your favourite book with us, the Muffin Man book, you were content! We took you to the Taiwanese night market every night and you slept in a cot beside our hotel bed. In Hualien, you took your first shower with your dad and loved rolling around your hotel bed naked.

When you were ten months old, you flew across the Pacific Ocean from Hong Kong to Vancouver like the bravest little baby boy. You never once cried on the journey, although it took at least twenty hours. In Vancouver, you started to become a healthier, stronger baby. You started saying *mama* and *dada* and it was beautiful. You spent the first two months in Vancouver with your grandma and grandpa, who came from Cambridge, Ontario, to help take care of you. Every day they played Chinese videos for you, took you for walks around Wesbrook Village, and made you delicious puréed food. They love you so much.

On your first birthday, we had a party for you with some of our closest friends. You cried when we all sang happy birthday because you are a quiet, sensitive boy. In this way, you take after both your father and me, who don't like a lot of noise. Already you have so many personality traits. You are curious, playful, focused, and sensitive. We marvel every day at all the things you do, like your ability to sit and play with blocks for hours. Happy first birthday, my Kai-bear! We love you more than anything in the world!

Love always,
your mom,
Sept 8, 2018

[border]

I am a fetus in my mother's womb when stories about refugees travelling to the Thai border reach her in Kampong Thom. My mother hears about people getting food and water in the camps, about some refugees being sponsored to live in France or America. Thousands leave every day, making the journey on foot, by bicycle, on tops of trucks. My parents hear about the three-hundred-kilometre route that goes from Kampong Thom to Svay Sisophon, and then on to Chumrum Thmei at the border of Cambodia and Thailand. They know the route is dangerous, filled with Vietnamese checkpoints, landmines, malaria, and wild animals in the jungle. They hear the stories about many refugees who have been driven back at the border by Thai soldiers firing at them.

My parents learn all this, and still they make the decision to go. They and my two brothers ride on top of a large oil truck alongside other families on the day-long journey to Svay Sisophon. The motion of the vehicle makes my mother nauseous, and she throws up many times along the way.

I have been in my mother's womb for eight months when my family prepares for the most dangerous leg of the journey from

Svay Sisophon to Chumrum Thmei. They pay local people to take them by bicycle and then on foot through the jungle. My mother rides on the back of a bicycle, and suddenly the cyclist stops. He says my mother is too heavy and demands she pay more. My mother begs him to take pity on her, and eventually he continues.

My family arrives at a checkpoint controlled by the Vietnamese army. Many Cambodian refugees are being stopped here. They search my father and find a letter in his pocket written in Chinese. It was sent to him by his father in Laos and contains instructions on how to get to the refugee camp in Thailand. It is the only correspondence my father has had with his father in almost five years. The guard cannot read the letter, but anything in the Chinese language is suspicious, as Vietnam is now at war with China.

My father is detained while my mother and two brothers have already crossed the checkpoint. My youngest brother screams and cries when he notices that my father has been stopped. The guard sees this and asks my father if the boy is his son. My father says no. *I don't know them. He is just a boy crying.* The guard lets my mother and brothers go on, but my father must stay and wait to be questioned further. When the guard is not looking, my father runs away, back into the jungle. It takes him two days to reach Chumrum Thmei, where he reunites with my mother and brothers. From here, they prepare for their next crossing, to Khao-I-Dang.

Refugee processing photo, Khao-I-Dang Holding Center, 1980.

[stories]

There is a story I heard growing up about Thai soldiers who shot at a Cambodian refugee woman as she held her newborn child in her arms. Later, a Red Cross vehicle came to the scene. After dispersing the soldiers scavenging her body for gold, they found the refugee woman unconscious but still alive, a bullet in her leg and her dead child in her arms.

The woman survived and eventually made it across the border to Thailand, and then to Canada, where she settled in the small town of Goderich, Ontario, the rural town where I grew up, and where I knew her as Toe, the mother of the only other Cambodian family in town. My memories of her are of an elegant, graceful woman with a prosthetic leg who could speak some English but mostly conversed in Khmer. After her escape, she had two children with a husband who had also left a family behind in Cambodia. One of her daughters, Nimual, was one of my best friends growing up. The refugee mother communicated her story to her daughter, who repeated it to me. The story tells of two absences: the child who perished at the border, and the mother's past as a dancer for the Royal Cambodian Ballet.

The last time I saw Toe's daughter, Nimual, I promised her that I would one day communicate her mother's story to others through the written page.

Promise me, Y-Dang. Promise me you will tell my mother's story.

[wounding]

My father remembers the first time he became a "boat person."

It is late 1973, seven years before I am born. He is on a cargo boat filled with hundreds of people making their way along the Tonle Sap River from the besieged town of Kampong Thom to Phnom Penh, a city beginning to swell with refugees. The highways have been cut off, controlled by the Khmer Rouge, so people have no choice but to travel to the capital by boat or by helicopter evacuation. My father is trying to reunite with my mother and two brothers, who were evacuated to Phnom Penh seven months earlier.

The journey by boat is dangerous. The Khmer Rouge are trying to stop the refugees from fleeing, so they hide in the coconut trees along the Tonle Sap. When the cargo boat goes around a bend in the river it slows, and Khmer Rouge soldiers fire from the treetops.

My father watches as people around him are shot, injured, and killed. He cannot believe he survives.

[big sounds]

In 1971, the war arrived in the city of Kampong Thom, as it had throughout Cambodia.

My father remembers how the sky was regularly filled with US military scanning drones and fighter jets. *We knew they were American because the Khmer Rouge and Lon Nol didn't have those kinds of machines.* Every day the drones circle above, quietly snapping aerial photographs, while the jets approach the city, roaring and shaking the earth. *The US planes didn't drop bombs directly on the city, but they came down very low and made a very big sound.* One day, when the sound of the jets becomes so constant it is deafening, my mother and father decide to take their two young children out of the city. They take shelter and sleep overnight in a Buddhist temple complex, a site rumoured to be safe from the US bombs.

When they return the next day, the US-backed Lon Nol army has taken over their home. During wartime, the army has the right to enter and use anyone's private property. The house is now filled with soldiers coming and going. Rockets fire from the rooftop. *The rockets would come every morning. People would lie*

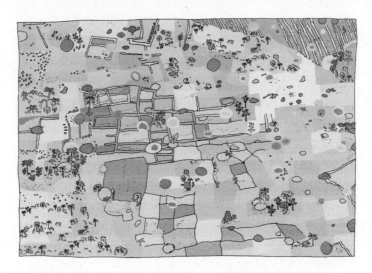

*Illustrated aerial view of a Cambodian landscape in the afterlife of the
Cold War in Cambodia: bomb ponds, kapok trees, and regrowth.
Illustration by Ulrike Zöllner, 2021. Courtesy of the artist.*

*Aerial view of craters made by US bombs, Kandal Province, Cambodia,
November 14, 2014. Kimlong Meng, CC BY-SA 4.0, via Wikimedia Commons.*

down on the streets. One morning, my father watches in horror as a rocket hits a man on the street, killing him on the spot. My father is standing so close to the blast that a piece of shrapnel wounds him on the neck.

The scar is still here, he says, pointing at his neck. *You can see it.*

[collapse]

In early 1975, my parents find themselves back in their hometown of Kampong Thom.

The war has reached a lull. The US jets and drones are no longer visible in the skies above; the rockets drop less frequently. The war seems to be coming to an end. My parents reopen their convenience supply store, which is now frequently visited by soldiers and generals of the Lon Nol army. These generals, who work closely with the CIA and the US military, accumulate a large tab every month, buying food, liquor, and cigarettes. My parents know some of these men are capable of horrible things, but some are also friends and neighbours.

In the weeks before April 17, 1975, my parents begin to notice a change in the air. Cambodian currency, the riel, starts to devalue and depreciate. People begin hoarding food and medicine, buying up everything in the supply store, paying more for the same item with each passing day. My mother and father hear that the Lon Nol soldiers are beginning to trade all their money for gold. Some gold stores are completely sold out. The pharmacies are empty. Fearful of what this could mean, my parents begin to make preparations.

They bury their valuables and money, *at least 5 million riel*, and wait for news of the war.

Two days before April 17, during the Khmer New Year celebrations, a captain in the Lon Nol army comes to the store to pay off his tab and urges my parents to leave Cambodia. The news has spread that the US is pulling out of Southeast Asia, that Phnom Penh will soon fall to the Khmer Rouge. The captain tells my parents about a planned US evacuation that will take place in twenty-four hours. *Those who have some connections, some ties to the US military, have an opportunity to leave and become refugees in America.* The evacuation will take place at hôtel khet, the army headquarters in town. My parents know this location well. Two years earlier, my mother and two brothers had been evacuated by helicopter from hôtel khet, leaving my father stranded at the last minute. My father remembers watching the helicopter lift off and away with his family, wondering if he would ever see them again. He does not have much faith in the evacuation this time.

The captain tells my mother and father that this time things will be different. The situation is grave, but he can get them out as a family. My mother makes the decision to stay.

We didn't know. We never imagined what Cambodia would become. That the world would change overnight. We thought the war was over. This is the biggest regret of my life. What we went through after, what your brothers went through—I'll never forgive myself.

At 8 a.m. the next day, the skies above fill with black helicopters, circling like a spiral of birds. At least ten of them swoop down to hôtel khet, pick up those on the evacuation list, and lift away.

[black holes]

My therapist asks me how it feels to carry this work, my research on Cambodia, with me for so many years. How consciously have I thought about the psychic effect of working so intimately with my family's stories? I struggle to answer him. I've confided in him about many other things, but this subject eludes me. I feel at a loss for words. How to express the effect of listening, reading, writing, and translating these accounts for a decade as a researcher, and for a lifetime as a daughter? The barrier between myself and the work sometimes feels so thin, the furthest thing from the lens of a neutral observer. I know there is a cost to knowing, but I don't know how this cost has been paid by me personally.

He asks me to identify the emotion. *Anger*, I say without hesitation. He asks me to visualize it. I tell him the anger is large, a force that's always moving. It's both a vortex and a void drawing in all my mental energy and thoughts, growing bigger with each passing year. The anger propels but debilitates. The more I know, the more the void expands. Eventually this dark place consumes everything I do, and then anger bleeds into feelings of sadness. I tell him one of the deepest pains I've felt over the past decade is the pain of failure. My scholarly book on Cambodia's history, art, and regeneration after the Khmer Rouge era, which I have been working on tirelessly for half a decade, was rejected by a press's editorial board, even after it was approved by anonymous reviewers and evaluators. In their rationale, the board stated my work was not academic enough, that its subjects—Cambodia's civil war, the US bombings, the Khmer Rouge takeover, work camps, genocide and its aftermaths—were too minor for a scholarly book, unless these issues were "ported" to speak to histories and places closer to the West. But their most devastating comment was that I, as an author, could not claim to be an expert on the subject matter—that is, on my own history. Dealing with and researching this history has overwhelmed me again and again. My book's rejection signals my failure to tell my family's stories, our history. I feel lost and disoriented. Lately, I say, I feel my brain disintegrating. I've become incapable of writing, except in short fragments.

My therapist tells me about the world-destroying vortices in Afrofuturism, the capacity of these vortices to swallow homes and cities, and the radical strength within this energy. I'm surprised he thinks of the force inside me as one of vitality. It feels to me as if this force is destroying me, piece by piece, year by year. He tells me a tale about a boy who puts the black hole into a box, opening the box carefully and slowly from time to time, but never closing it for good. He says I can do this too.

I fear the consequence of doing this. I don't know if words are carrying me or swallowing me.

A good topic. The initial presentation of the book is confusing, and even disconcerting. It focuses on "cultural disappearance," but the topic is the consequences following the killing of artists and cultural producers. The result is an unintentional diminishment of the significance of the killings themselves, as they become subordinate to the effects on the production of cultural objects. I think culture is a serious topic, god knows, but Troeung needs to acknowledge the importance of the killings themselves in her introduction, so the book doesn't appear to care more about art than life . . . I'm not sure the author quite recognizes the centrality of the problem.

—Book Rejection Letter #1 from an anonymous
editorial board member

It's a great topic and its findings are potentially portable to other cases of art and trauma studies (Ireland, Greece, Syria, etc.). But the narrow focus is not helping, nor the intellectual myopia. More theory, more subtle use of theory, could help ventilate the project beyond the silo it's currently inhabiting.

—Book Rejection Letter #2 from an anonymous
editorial board member

[remembrance]

November 11, 2018. My one-year-old son is in the hospital, hooked up to a rattling IV. It has been the longest day of my life.

I drove here like a madwoman this morning, convinced that my son, lifeless and limp in the car seat behind me, was dead. I could not call an ambulance because I had left my cellphone at the same hospital's emergency room the night before, when I was afraid his fever had reached deadly highs. I blamed myself for not forcing the nurses to register him then, for a million things, for everything. I saw my life haunted by a loss for which I was at fault.

It's dark now in the hospital room. Chris, my husband, is sleeping. Kai, too, is mercifully asleep. It's the first moment of quiet I've had in many hours—more than forty-eight, I would say. I hear Kai stir.

Today happens to be Remembrance Day. Growing up, I was told to remember the soldiers who fought in wars across the seas. I always thought it was strange to be told to remember something that didn't happen to me, something far outside my own memory. What do we, the survivors of war, the refugees, remember?

November 11, 1978

My parents and brothers are on the verge of dying. It's a miracle if they live.

November 11, 1988

I'm eight years old. We live in a small town in Canada called Goderich. Happiness is fragile. My mother's screams pierce the air, fill the house, always.

November 11, 1998

My family sits around our kitchen table as we joyously pore over the acceptance letters I've received to every university I've applied for. I am ready to channel all my energy in one direction.

November 11, 2008

I'm in Cambodia with my mother, researching my uncle's disappearance. I meet my Cambodian family, whom my mother has not seen in over thirty years. I go back to the beginning. Then further back, forever turning.

November 11, 2011

It's the day of my Ph.D. dissertation defence, the final hoop. My eldest brother is in jail, arrested for associating with people whom the police call gangsters. My family is imploding. It's very difficult to concentrate.

November 10, 2018

My students in Canada debate Remembrance Day. Some want to wear a white poppy, others the red one. That night, my son has a seizure. I rush him to emergency.

November 11, 2018

I feel as if it's all added up to here, all the years, all the deaths, the illnesses, the losses. They all add up and up and up.

Dearest Kai,

It has taken me until October to write this. Around the time of your birthday, mama had to go away for a week to Cambodia. She really, really did not want to leave you, but there was an important conference she felt she could not miss. Like your father, she has found it very difficult to leave your side ever since your health emergencies over the past year.

Last November, while your father attended a conference, you had a seizure. I found you unconscious. Alone, I drove you to the hospital in the middle of the night, nearly colliding with the few other cars on the road. At the hospital, I was terrified. A nurse sat me down, placed a warm blanket on my shoulders and comforted me. When your father came back the next day, I was able to let go of the panic. We had no idea what was wrong with you, and the mystery of your sickness gnawed at us for the next three months until January, when it happened again. You vomited, then screamed, then shook in belly-fits, then you passed out again. We called 911 and firemen came, then medics, then police, and your father sat with you in the ambulance and texted me that your eyes had begun to open.

After those two week-long hospitalizations, I was on edge every time I put you to sleep. I remember sometimes just sitting up all night by your bedside, watching you sleep, worried that something might happen if I let my guard down. When you were congested and had difficulty breathing throughout the night, I would sometimes climb into your crib and rest you on my chest. Your father joked that I became a *human recliner*, sitting up halfway if you needed to decongest, lying down again when you fell asleep.

At home, I could comfort you like this, instead of sitting up all night in the cold, hard chair by your hospital bed, seeing you hooked up to so many wires, so small and frail in your pink-and-white gown. I was tormented by the sound of the IV dripping, dripping, and dripping. The nurses had to come take your blood every four hours, waking you up and making you cry out in pain. *Is it necessary to take so much blood?* I cried out once in frustration. It was agony. I cried on your father's shoulder in disbelief that you had to endure this.

After a few days, I had to leave the room every time they took your blood. I couldn't take it anymore. Thank god for your dada, who was calm and strong, who could stand above your crib and squeeze your little hand while the nurse drew vials of blood. I marvelled at his strength of mind in these moments. How he took care of me emotionally, how he reached out to our friends to remind us we weren't alone, how he even managed to teach his classes by video conferencing from your hospital-room bathroom!

In the end, brave little Kai, we were able to go home together, and I was able to breathe at last. My brightest memory from this time was when you were strong enough to go for a walk in the forest.

Bouncing along on your dada's chest in a little baby-carrier, you stared wide-eyed at the rainforest of majestic old-growth trees. Your father and I called the Pacific Spirit *the healing forest*. We breathed the fresh air, marvelled at the *mother trees*, and wondered if it was true that these trees communicated with each other through an underground network. With their roots sprawling and twisting above the ground, the mother trees reminded me of the ancient trees at Angkor Wat in Cambodia. One day, I hope, you will see the trees of Angkor, like I once did, as the repository of the deep time of our ancestors, the witnesses to suffering and rebirth, and one of the most beautiful places on Earth. Like you, those trees are strong and enduring. They remind me that anything is possible.

In March, the doctors gave you a diagnosis that had been suggested in Hong Kong but was very difficult to verify. Only one in sixty thousand children has it. Our pediatrician said that your health problems would get easier after you turned two. You'd have more body fat to keep you from low blood sugar.

The next six months we took your blood sugar and spent hours making your food as appetizing as possible. You lost your front teeth. We had to give you a needle injection every night, which you bravely endured. We turned it into a game called "needle-time!" We felt terrible every time we tried to give you more food and you wouldn't eat it. How could we explain that this was going to keep you alive?

It's October now, and you have remarkable health. Our pediatrician was right, things have got easier. Before you were born, in our more carefree days living in Hong Kong, your father and I would have travelled alone to two or three countries within the month of September, speaking at conferences and having romantic nights out. But now, to stay in our new home with you, without doctors or hospitals, or any worries about doctors and hospitals, feels like the first true vacation we've ever had.

You will probably not remember the past year. But you might see me worrying about you. You might see me getting flashbacks of the hospital, and you may not know why sometimes I will need to curl up with you and watch TV and let you do whatever you want because you're alive and that's a miracle.

Love always,
your mom,
October 2, 2019

Front page of the Montreal Gazette, *December 4, 1980. A human interest story about my family's arrival in Canada and my first look at snow.*

[country]

When Alice Munro won the Nobel Prize for Literature in 2013, I couldn't help but feel a twinge of pride that a writer from the place *where I am from* had received such worldwide recognition. This place where I am from is often referred to as "Alice Munro Country."

After spending nearly all the first year of my life in my birth-place, camp Khao-I-Dang, I spent the next seventeen years in Goderich, Ontario. The wide-open spaces of the forest, the roads, and the lake shaped my identity, made me feel free to eat, sleep, and try new things, anywhere I pleased. When I was old enough to read Alice Munro, I was immediately immersed in the world of her stories. Goderich, a remote town known for its salt-mine industry and its famous tractors, often appears in Munro's fiction disguised as Walley or Tupperton. Somehow, in the turmoil of my adolescence and the alienation I felt as one of only a few Asians in a town of seven thousand people, I took refuge in Munro's tales of family betrayal, sexual rebellion, and the strangeness of familiar places. Hiding away reading in a corner of the public library in town, I was carried away by how Munro portrayed the landscapes, rhythms, and feelings of my own small-town life. Munro was well-known for drawing inspiration from historical sources. My family's story has made national headlines and is in history books. I often wondered if our story would ever make it into her fiction.

In many small towns across Huron County, from Goderich to Vanastra to Exeter, there have lived many Cambodian, Lao, and Vietnamese families who crossed the Pacific as refugees. Within our communities, stories circulate about the forms of kindness shown to us by our sponsors, as well as the cruel forms of hate and aggression we have had to steel ourselves against. I often imagine our stories put to the page, stories of humour and gossip and bitter divisions, just as in Munro's work.

The line "Who do you think you are?" was the title of one of my favourite Munro collections, about a rebellious girl named Rose who leaves her small town for Toronto. I identified with Rose, her careful intelligence, her constant questioning. Her story expressed my own longings for escape.

Now, over twenty years since I left Goderich, I have stopped waiting for stories like mine and my family's to be written by the national artists. When, little by little, these stories do emerge, they come from refugees who write in poems and fragments. We, the children of refugees, let the stories we never could write drop through our fingers.

[labour]

1980. My family of five resettle in Goderich. In an instant, my mother and father set aside their grief and get to work.

With three children to support, my parents take on multiple day jobs: factory work, piecework sewing, apple picking, baby-sitting. One evening, my mother comes home from work at the local factory, the Sheaffer Pen Company, in tears. Her co-workers had called her a *slave driver* for working so hard and making them look bad. New to the English language, she does not understand the meaning of this term, *slave driver*. She asks me to explain it to her. A child, I do not understand the term's meaning myself. *It's the person who drives the slaves to work*, I say, and my mother shakes her head in confusion.

One day, my father comes home from work at the local trailer manufacturing plant, General Coach, frustrated and limping in pain from an ankle injury he acquired on the job. He tells me that a plant foreman stood behind him all day with a timer, telling him to work faster, asking him if he had *a pulse*. My father asks me, what does *pulse* mean? I know from school that having a pulse means that you are alive. My father scoffs and says his foreman is just like the Khmer Rouge, cracking bayonets over people's heads if they stopped working fast enough. He knows the type. The foreman won't be satisfied until my father is worked to death.

[produce]

Whenever I am reminded that the majority of Canadians did not want to take in refugees at the time of our arrival, I am also reminded that refugees provide an *economic boon* for the nation that did not want us, and that statistics can prove this. I've heard this called *the economic argument* for refugee resettlement.

When I was growing up, my family never went on vacation; we never had this thing called *leisure*. Instead, we were expected to embody debt, to pay back the country hosting us, through an unceasing willingness to work. We could not be idle but had to keep overcoming all kinds of pain and hardship, no longer in pursuit of survival but of economic success.

Even as I write these words, I do not do so idly. To write my own story, I must first create conditions for myself so that these written words will be, in some way, outside the demands of productivity.

[home]

There is a scene I remember vividly from my childhood. I am around eight years old, sitting at the kitchen window in our home in Goderich. This is my favourite spot because I can observe everything happening outside. In this new country, my parents say, there is so much space for everyone. Even poor refugees like us can live in a house with a driveway long enough to park four cars front to back.

Beside our house is a vast, empty grass field owned by the lumber company next door. With all this outdoor space, my brothers spend countless hours outside playing ball hockey, basketball, soccer, and baseball. I know that very soon my brothers will arrive home from high school and likely start a game of one-on-one basketball, using the net set up at the end of the driveway. If they're feeling generous, they will let me join their game for a few minutes and teach me to do a layup or shoot a three-pointer.

My parents work long hours at their factory jobs, but they are still always back in time to have a home-cooked dinner ready for us. These days, we don't have to set out for the graveyard anymore to pick worms after dark, as we did in the early years of our arrival in Canada. After eight years, my parents have saved up enough money to pay a mortgage, own a car, and put food on the table for us three kids. Today, I hear them working outside the house, chatting calmly as they go through their yardwork routines.

My mother screams. I hear my father's distressed tones, and I know something is wrong. I go outside and see my parents holding up my oldest brother, who has come home alone. They ask him repeatedly, *Who did this?* There are bruises on his face, blood visible on his head and hands. How he managed to stumble home on his own is a wonder. He is clearly in pain but not crying or trembling. He stands perfectly still. My parents try to hold him, comfort him somehow. My mother sobs. The look in my father's eyes is red-blooded anger.

My father goes to the police station. He is a gentle, soft-spoken man, and in all the years of my childhood, I have never seen him as angry as he is on this day. He tells the police that two older teenagers, two brothers, followed his son after school and attacked him from behind. They had been bullying him for weeks with taunts and racial slurs. *Go back to where you came from, Chink!* Today, the brothers caught him walking home alone, pushed him to the sidewalk, and beat him mercilessly. Had it been a fair fight, the bullies would not have had a chance. During Pol Pot's time, my brother won many fights, toiled in the sun doing hard labour, scavenged for food, walked for days in the jungle and mountains. My mother had always described him as *the tough one*. With my father sent away for months at a time to work, it was my brother who had to take care of the family. He had always protected his younger brother, the weaker and more sickly child in the family. Now, in Canada, things are different. It is my oldest brother who is targeted. It is he who needs protection.

My father demands to know what the police are going to do. If they won't do anything, my father says, he will take matters into his own hands. *Do you know what my son has been through before coming here? Do you know?* The police tell my father to calm down. They say they will take care of things, and they send him home.

Hours later many people gather in our driveway. The police have arrived with the parents of the bullies. Our sponsors, who are my brother's godparents, have arrived to act as mediators. A long discussion ensues, with the townspeople mostly talking to each other in English. The parents of the bullies apologize to my parents on behalf of their sons. The father is a taxi driver, known to many in town. It is decided that charges will not be laid. The sponsors advise my parents that this is the best thing to do. *Let things be*, they say. *It is a small town, and we have our own ways of doing things here.* I observe this discussion up close, peeking out shyly from behind my father's legs.

I see my brother, stone-faced, watching us from my favourite spot at the kitchen window, where you can see everyone outside, but remain hidden in the dark.

My family at Phanat Nikhom Refugee Camp in Chonburi Province, Thailand, October 10, 1980. My eldest brother, Meng, stands between my mother and my youngest brother, Pheng. Phanat Nikhom was the largest holding camp in Thailand for Southeast Asian refugees who had been cleared for resettlement.

[bat]

In the weeks that follow the after-school attack in Goderich, my brother carries a baseball bat with him everywhere. His armour and his weapon, the bat will protect him. He is no longer afraid. He is a teenager by Canadian standards, but has already been living, fighting, for what feels like a full lifetime. He hears the stories about two Vietnamese refugees in the neighbouring town of Clinton who got into a fight with the locals at a bar one night. The locals beat them badly, but the Vietnamese came back another night, this time with all their refugee friends.

My father hears about the fallout from the bar fight in Clinton. Some of the locals were badly injured, and some of the Vietnamese were being sent to jail. The case is all over the news. My father is worried because his half-brother, a "paper son" from Laos, has been getting involved with these refugee gangs. My father sees clearly where things are going. The situation is fragile. Soon they will come for his boys. He forbids my brother from doing anything, tells him to put the bat away. My brother obeys but does not forget. He can never forget the searing pain, the look of horror in my mother's eyes, my father's indignity and fear.

Many years later, my brother chuckles when I ask him about the baseball bat he carried around in his trunk for years. He tells me that, funnily enough, he saw his bully not that long ago in a bar. The bully merely nodded at him from across the room, as if they were casual friends.

I felt it all coming back right away. That anger, that rage. Maybe I would have said something, done something, but you know I'm a father now. I can't be that way anymore.

[easter epic]

April 18, 1987. Tonight is a special night. It's the NHL playoffs—game seven of the division semifinals. There is always excitement in our home during playoff nights. Watching hockey, along with eating and playing cards, is our favourite family pastime. We spend hours every week watching hockey on our small television in the living room. Our house is never still or quiet. There is laughter, television, music, and people coming and going all the time.

I am eight years old and in another of my favourite spots. This one is in the living room, beneath a desk built into the wall in the corner. I can see and hear everything in the living room: the hockey game on TV, the yellow water stains on the ceiling, the sheets of rain pouring down outside, my brothers jumping off the couch and yelling out at the screen.

Ooohhh, nice pass!

What was that?!

That should be a penalty!

In just seven short years in Canada, my brothers have transformed themselves into small-town Canadian boys. Determined not to be mistaken for *out-of-townies*, they absorb all the town has to offer. Football, soccer, hockey, Ozzy Osbourne, Heart, Journey, euchre, the beach, the Square, the gravel runs, the parties, the orchards, and the graveyards. During the playoffs, my brothers join hockey pools with their friends and make bets against each other. They let me get involved too, giving me the important job of keeping track of all the points on a large piece of white bristol board.

Two points for a goal, one for an assist. Got it?

From the living room to the kitchen, I run back and forth, grabbing us Cokes, chips, and green mangoes with chili salt. As the game goes on, my mother and father bring in real food to keep us going—fried rice, spring rolls, and lemongrass chicken wings. We devour it all, feeling like life couldn't be happier.

During the playoffs, my older brother likes to wear the hockey jersey of his favourite team, the Montreal Canadiens, or the Habs, as everyone calls them. In this qualifying round, the Canadiens will be playing the Boston Bruins. That ancient rivalry. From my brother, I've learned everything I need to know to love the Habs, and together we hate the Bruins.

Patrick Roy is the best goalie who ever lived.

Chris Chelios, such an enforcer, man!

Ray Bourque is a dork!

But tonight, the Saturday night of Easter long weekend, we are watching two other legendary rivals face off: the Washington Capitals versus the New York Islanders. We cheer for the Capitals because the Islanders have already won the Cup four times since we've come to Canada. The Habs, the underdogs, will have a better chance if the Islanders get eliminated now. The game is thrilling. I am biting my nails. It goes back and forth, back and forth, and when the third period reaches an end, the game is tied.

My brothers are on the edge of their seats—but the television is switched off. The spring evening has brought a big rainfall, and everyone knows it's time to head out. We might only have a few hours left to pick the worms we need at the cemetery. My brothers want nothing more than to stay home and watch the game in over-time. All their friends will be talking about it when school resumes on Tuesday.

It's time to go, my father says, and my brothers don't protest. They know what they must do. With their small hands and sharp eyes, they can pick much faster than my parents.

They are good boys, my mother and father always say.

My brother changes out of his Habs jersey into dark clothes that will blend into the night. Lately police officers have been coming around to clear out the worm-picking refugees from the cemeteries. Best not to wear anything that might attract the cops.

At the cemetery, my mother, father, and brothers set out with tin cans strapped to their ankles and headlamps on their heads. I want to help too, but my mother says I'm still too young. She tells me to stay in the car and lock the doors. Normally I keep the doors locked anyway so the ghosts can't get in, but tonight I roll down the windows a crack. The air is fresh with the smell of rain, and I can hear my brothers' excited chatter mingle with the tinkling of their ankle-cans.

The ref should've called a penalty!

Yeah, they got robbed!

Trottier, man, he was good.

I hear them laughing and goofing around. Once in a while, one of them finds a worm the size of a snake and yells out, *Hey check this one out. It's as big as Potvin!* They throw worms back and forth as if they're having a snowball fight. From my spot in the car's back seat, I watch them play among the ghosts.

We drive back home hours later with a trunk full of square wooden crates packed with worms. Each crate carries a toss of sawdust to keep the worms alive. Would the worms be sold for fishing bait? As raw material for lipstick? We would never know. My mother's and father's joints ache and their hands are raw with cold, but it was all worth it.

My father always describes the worms as gold. Each ankle-can contains around one hundred worms, and on a great night they can fill ten cans. This night produced a good haul—one hundred dollars' worth of worms, perhaps. Everyone is happy. When we get home, my mother tells me to go to bed. She reminds me that we have to go to church in the morning. It's Easter Sunday, and everyone will expect us to be there.

I hear a commotion coming from the living room. The television is on, and my older brother is calling my younger brother to hurry and come watch. *The game is still going! They're in quadruple overtime!* None of us can believe it.

This hockey game will go down as the longest game seven in NHL history—the Easter Epic. My brothers, bone-tired but thrilled, stand right in front of the TV, their clothes still damp. I hear frying and sizzling in the kitchen. I curl up with my blanket on the couch and hope the magical night never ends.

[worms]

I ask my parents about their worm-picking days. I learn that the worms they and my brothers picked in wet graveyards would later be sold to fishermen in informal networks across Ontario.

My father seems flustered as he details the level of co-operation between the Southeast Asian refugees who were picking worms and the local community. In order to gain legal access to places like the private cemetery, golf courses, and farms, my family had to get letters of permission in advance. They would show these whenever the police would come by to investigate. My family's private sponsors helped us get these letters, and sometimes one of our sponsors (a Lebanese Canadian woman named Laurie) would come down to help with the worm-picking. As my father says, *At that time, people were still nice to refugees. They helped us so we could go pick gold.*

The work was lucrative (especially on nights of heavy rain in May and June), and we could earn fifty to a hundred dollars per night as a family. The church, by comparison, provided seventy-five dollars per week to my family for our first two years of resettlement. My parents believed that every Southeast Asian refugee family in southeast Western Ontario was involved in this work throughout the 1980s. This subterranean economy spanned from Goderich to Toronto, where the worms were shipped out to the US.

[diaspora]

Years later, I share my parents' story of worm-picking with a group of Cambodian Americans I meet in Phnom Penh. They are all around my age and we talk about our families' extraordinary ability to find ways of surviving after resettlement.

Growing up, I tell them, *my family had an odd night job: picking worms.* I tell the story with my mother's dramatic tinge. *After a big rainfall, our home would be filled with an air of anticipation. Before midnight, my parents would gather me and my brothers, and drive us all down to the cemetery.* I tell the story with the same care for detail as my father. I remember the clinking sounds of the tin cans my family tied around their ankles, the bright white glare of the lamps they affixed to their heads, and the excited chatter about how many boxes they might fill. I tell my own version of the story, of being left alone in the car, but feeling unafraid. How I would gaze out the window into the darkness of the cemetery and feel comforted by the dance of headlamps made by the upward and downward swoops of my family's work. I tell them about a common experience we all have of facing the police. *One night, a police car approached us in the cemetery, and my father showed them a letter of permission. "We have permission to work here at night," my father said firmly. "Here is the letter from our sponsor."*

The other children of refugees share stories gathered from their parents and their own memories. They talk of picking mushrooms, fishing for clams, of obtaining whatever the earth had available in the various regions across the US. We tell our stories, then stories we've heard from others. I tell them that a man once told me about a Cambodian family he knew who could spot and pick edible things in the bushes near the sidewalks of a Los Angeles suburb.

After a night of storytelling, while I am inside a tuk-tuk on my way back to the hotel, I wonder if my parents worried about offending the spirits of the dead as they walked across grave plots searching for gold. Did they know that a cemetery was a sacred place in Catholicism, their new adopted religion? Did any of the refugees who picked worms, from Goderich to Exeter to Toronto, fear rousing the dead?

I feel something binding me to these stories, and to the children of refugees who have shared their own with me. The stories evoke intense admiration at the ingenuity of our parents' survival, as well as a deep pain at the scale and intensity of their loss.

Production still from Easter Epic. *Courtesy of the author.*

[frame]

I am sitting in the garage of a rented house that has been re-made into an elaborate 1980s film set. I watch our prop manager rearrange framed pictures of me and my family. She and thirty others have gathered here to help me make a short film called *Easter Epic*, about one of the many nights my family picked worms. It has been a dream of mine to make a film. I have taught courses on film, and hosted university film festivals that featured films by hundreds of my own students. But this is the first time I've made one about my own story.

This collaborative process of filmmaking has awakened memories long in hibernation. For decades, I had relied on the memories of my family picking worms to give me strength and laughter, to remember a time, as my father says, when people were still nice to refugees. Deprived of leisure or vacation, we created our own magic. We turned hardship into opportunity, labour into fun, worms into gold. But reliving this time through the actors has brought back memories that my mind once suppressed. I remem-ber my parents feeling guilty that we didn't get to be like other kids who could stay home and watch hockey. I remember feeling uneasy watching my parents struggle to make ends meet, and wishing to do anything I could to help them.

One moment stings like a venom releasing into my memory. I recall, one afternoon, moving crates of worms into a basement cellar, when a tall white woman approached me. In her mind, I suppose, she had come to help a young girl all alone in an outdoor basement. But when she saw me carrying a crate full of live, writhing worms, she gave me a disgusted look and walked away. In that moment, this activity of worm-picking, which gave my family joy, pride, and needed income, became an object of shame.

I listen to the commotion on my film set. It's a whole-family affair. My parents consult with the actors, showing them how to chop mangoes and how to pronounce words in Khmer. My co-director Alejandro, a son of Chilean refugees and Japanese immigrants, readies the set for the next scene. Our costume designer comes from my hometown, Goderich. One of the makeup artists, a son of Vietnamese refugees from Cambridge, Ontario, told me on the second day of shooting that his father used to pick worms, as did many in his extended family. In the background, my son runs around with his father, laughing, until a voice shouts, "Quiet on set!"

The process of making this film is as I've always dreamed: a magical gathering of artists and outcasts channelling their passions into creating something beautiful. Like my parents after a long night of worm-picking, I feel proud of the work we have accomplished together. But as soon as I feel this, I remember her: the woman who stood at the top of the cellar stairway, looking upon me in disgust.

[old days]

My father and mother remember the old days in Cambodia, the time before the war. They call this period *ros ne yang sok sabai*, the years of happy living, when the country was relatively peaceful. It's a time full of colour, sound, smell, and touch.

My parents are young and in love. At my mother's home, the smell of grilled fish, mangoes, coconut, and sour fish soup wafts through the air. My father's home is filled with books, an entire library upstairs. Music plays constantly in the background: the Taiwanese love ballads of Teresa Teng and Zhang Xiao Ying; the Khmer rock 'n' roll of Sinn Sisamouth, Ros Serey Sothea, Pan Ron, and Chum Kem; the American music of Elvis Presley. My father remembers the story of how Chum Kem left Cambodia to study abroad.

Chum Kem didn't go away to study music, but when he came back he started to teach people the twist. He wrote "Kampuchea Twist" and young people started doing the twist and the ramvong. Your mother and I, we loved this music.

Not yet married, my parents keep their love an open secret. My father, a free spirit, is not favoured by my mother's family.

She has many suitors but is drawn to my father's passion for the arts. To escape the watchful eyes of others, they take the bus from Kampong Thom to Phnom Penh on the weekends.

In the capital, they are truly free! They go to the Central Market for *kuay teo* and Khmer iced coffee with condensed milk; they wander the Riverside and gaze at the other lovers. Most of all, they spend their time together eating out and going to see all the new movies playing at the theatres. They recall how the movies arrived in waves: first came the Shaw Brothers films from Hong Kong starring *kung fu* stars Wang Yu (王羽), Chiang Da-wei (姜偉年), Ti Lung (譚富榮), and Lee Xiao Long (李小龙); then came the epic movies from India—tales of the gods such as *Preah Vishnu* and *Preah Hanuman*; after a while, Cambodians started to make their own movies—adaptations of famous legends such as *Mak Thoeung*, *Moranak Meada*, and *Puos Keng Kang*, starring the great Cambodian actors Dy Saveth, Kim Nova, Kong Som Eun, and Saksi Sbong.

On these date nights, my mother wears bell-bottom pants and a long flower-print shirt, or sometimes jean shorts and a white cut-off top. Her hair is cut in the chic omega style. My father wears blue jeans and a Montagut striped shirt imported from France. He carries his Kodak SLR camera everywhere and snaps photos of their adventures all over Phnom Penh. His friend in Kampong Thom owns a photography studio and helps them develop hundreds of photos that they store in large albums.

When the Khmer Rouge arrive in 1975, my parents hide these photo albums under a mattress and never see them again. *A record of the happy times*, my father says, *but one day, suddenly, it was all gone.*

The Rising Phoenix. *Phnom Penh, Cambodia, 2014.*
Photo by FONKi. Courtesy of the photographer.

[walking]

When I was growing up, and still to this day, I've noticed something peculiar every time my mother tells a stranger that our family came to Canada as refugees from Cambodia. When she says *Cambodia*, her eyes drop and her voice softens, as if she hopes the word will not be heard. She knows that for most people, Cambodia is only a place where horrible things happened. There has been no other way of relating her experience, except through this narrow script of how tragic her life was in Cambodia and how lucky she feels to be in Canada. Over time, I've come to see my mother's difficulty in speaking about Cambodia (beyond the repetition of familiar soundbites) as a kind of debilitating silence shaped by the lack of space for her story to genuinely move within the world. Cambodia has burrowed inward, along with her pain, into the depths of her being. This burden of silence filled our entire household when I was growing up, covering every aspect of our lives like a thin layer of dust that would settle again moments after being brushed away.

Since returning to Canada in 2018, after living for six years in Hong Kong, I've been asking my mother more questions about the past, and listening to new stories or new versions of the same stories that have begun to flow out of her. One day, as we stand in my kitchen in Vancouver washing dishes, she starts recounting a memory I've never heard.

She describes walking through the forest by herself one day in 1976 and gazing up at the tall trees. She thinks of ending her life. In just one short year, she has lost her mother and two older brothers. Not knowing the exact details of how they were killed, she can only imagine gruesome scenes over and over in her mind. She feels overwhelmed by grief and despair, and thinks of joining her family in death. But then her thoughts drift to her two young children, my brothers. She wonders who would take care of them, if not her. She reminds herself that they need a mother to carry them through this world turned upside down, even as the end of the nightmare seems nowhere in sight. She looks ahead and continues walking through the forest.

[kamleang chet]

While telling the story of the forest, my mother describes her will to continue living using the Khmer words *kamleang chet*, meaning *strength of the heart*. She translates this concept for me as emotional survival, turning inward, mental willpower, not giving up. The will to survive in Pol Pot time, she explains, involved knowing when to remain silent, how to take one's mind elsewhere, how to disappear within oneself. It also involved knowing what to do and what to say at the right time.

My mother offers an example.

Living in the camps, each night she and my father listen and wait for the Khmer Rouge cadres to arrive at their huts. The Khmer Rouge move quietly outside, eavesdropping on people's private conversations. When my mother and father know the cadres are listening, they begin their nightly conversation. They talk about the importance of their individual sacrifice for the cause of the revolution, about the need to win the war, about the strength of the regime. They reminisce about a past they have never lived, fabricating memories that conceal their family ties. They do not call each other by their real names; they do not speak their native

Chinese language, *guoyu* (国语). They become experts at the art of invention. When they are sure that the Khmer Rouge are no longer listening, they stop talking at last. Sometimes, they are allowed to rest until dawn, and then the day's cycle repeats again. To survive Pol Pot time, my parents would say, *yeaung ban kamleang chet*: we had to have strength of the heart.

Because I grew up listening to my parents' accounts of *kamleang chet*, I was astonished and disoriented when I first came across all the prevailing images and films of Pol Pot time that focused so sharply on human skulls and mass graves. My inherited knowledge of the war was so vastly different, and I began to understand my mother's hesitation, her lowered breath, whenever she mentioned the word *Cambodia* to non-refugees. I began to see how Pol Pot time was not the end of their need to present themselves carefully and artfully to whoever might be listening.

[baksbat]

I often find myself wondering how, after Pol Pot time, my parents were able to come back to themselves. What selves were even left to go back to? If *kamleang chet* could be passed down, could their broken selves be transmitted as well?

The Khmer concept of *baksbat* translates as *broken courage* or *broken form*. I prefer the latter, *broken form*, because it invokes a sense of fragmented surface and impermanence. Breaking of the body is not necessarily the same as broken strength or broken spirit. Also, just because a form breaks does not mean it is broken, nor that it has become something shameful, incomprehensible, a thing to be silenced and forgotten.

I find these words in Khmer can express the brokenness of our selves in ways that give us repair and much-needed spiritual guidance. They attend to the impact of Pol Pot time on the collective and individual soul—what Cambodians call *pralung*. Pol Pot time was a spiritual rupture in which the *pralung* had disappeared from the body. Practices like *hau pralung* (recalling the soul) rituals are performed during periods of transition, rites of passage, illness, or after staying in a foreign land. Our souls wander, become wayward spirits, but our rituals invite them back into their proper seat within the body.

I struggle to find a perfect language to define the conditions I am living in, and that of my parents. Perhaps I rely too much on definitions, when so often the speech of refugees is met only with the silence of an unreceptive public.

There is one English word that I rely upon to understand my family's history, a word that recalls both security and security forces, a word that brings comfort as much as it does madness, a word that erects houses for refugee families as well as prisons to house their children. This is the word *asylum*, a word that means both a sanctuary for the displaced and a ward for the mentally ill, both the entanglement of refugee-ness and the madness of war. When I hear this word, I feel lightning—it is so precise, even if no one else knows what I am hearing.

Yes, I say. *My family was granted asylum.*

[hometown]

My mother often tells a story about how she saved my father.

It is 1976, four years before I am born. My family lives in a *pom*, a village in the jungle created by clearing brush and building huts made of bamboo. My father is sent out to work in a co-operative of about fifteen other men. My mother, a woman of twenty-eight, stays at home with my brothers, who are around eight and nine. It takes my father and his workgroup two days to walk to the work-site through dense jungle. Many cannot endure the unremitting labour, the harsh tropical elements, and the lack of food. One by one, people die of exhaustion and illness. Weeks later, only about five men return to the *pom*. My father is not among them.

Hearing rumours that my father is ill, my mother begs the village leader to let her go see him. *Most Khmer Rouge leaders are cruel, but some have a kind heart.* This cadre feels pity for my mother and gives her a transit letter to walk to the worksite to see about my father. She walks for days, by herself, through the jungle, foraging for food along the way, stopping to rest and to sleep on the earth. When she arrives at the worksite, she finds my father gravely ill. *He was left outside under a tree, where they left people to die.* He is unconscious, on the brink of death, but his heart still beats. She pleads with the work co-operative leader to transport my father to a hospital in Kampong Thom. *Please, look, he's still alive*, she says. Eventually they agree to transport him. The vehicle arrives full of Khmer Rouge soldiers. They stop my mother from entering the vehicle. They point a rifle at her and order her to stop. *I got down on my knees and begged them to let me go with him. When they still refused, I stood up and screamed at them: You kill me, kill me. You shoot me, then I die, I don't care! But I will go with him!*

Dumbfounded, the Khmer Rouge soldiers give in and allow my mother to board. She travels in the vehicle with them, protecting my father's unconscious body.

The city of Kampong Thom, her hometown, is barely recognizable—a ghost town, almost empty. The hospital is scarcely a hospital. The sick and dying lie on hard, flat wooden beds. Some patients are given basic IVs, but modern medicine is not available. My mother sits on the floor at my father's bedside waiting for him to regain consciousness. She thinks of her children back at the *pom*, sent out daily to work in the children's work co-operative. She thinks of her youngest son, who is frail and showing signs of dysentery. *How much longer can he survive?* She leans her head against the side of the bed to rest.

Two or three days pass before my father finally stirs. He slowly regains consciousness, but it will be three months before he leaves the hospital. My mother cannot stay. She must return to her children. She makes the journey on foot, alone, through the jungle. It takes her an entire day to walk back to the *pom*.

No one would believe how people survived in Pol Pot time, she tells me.

[wandering soul]

My mother tells me a story about how her mother, a superstitious woman and devout Buddhist, was once visited by a fortune teller in the years before wartime. The fortune teller foretold of a gap, a dark time in Cambodia, that would take place when my grandmother was sixty years old. If she could cross this gap, her life would be spared and she would go on to live for many more years.

In 1976, during the dark time that the fortune teller foretold, my grandmother was sent to work in the forest with a group of three other elderly people. As my parents often explained to me, during Pol Pot time, people were grouped according to their age and gender: men, women, children, and the elderly worked separately. My brothers were sent out to work in the children's brigades; my mother primarily worked in rice planting; my father was usually sent out to construct dikes, dams, and canals. On some occasions, he was sent to destroy Buddhist temples.

One day, my grandmother's mobile unit was ordered to go into a forest to cut grass that would be used for roofing. All the locals knew that this forest was under the domain of Lok Ta, a powerful guardian spirit that no one dared offend. Everyone knew

Lok Ta protected the area, but he could also be a dangerous spirit (all guardian spirits, *neak ta*, were this way in Cambodia). You had to ask permission from Lok Ta before you could pick anything. You had to say something at least. If you did not believe, you just did not go in.

After working in this forest, my grandmother fell critically ill, as did the three other people in her work unit. The villagers whispered that they had made Lok Ta angry, that the Khmer Rouge sent them there on purpose. My mother remembered the fortune teller's omen.

My mother's last image of my grandmother was of her being taken away by the Khmer Rouge. Because she was sixty years old, considered elderly, she was of no use to the regime. They did not entertain the idea of taking her to the hospital in the city of Kampong Thom. The cadres said she was being taken to the village hospital, but she was never seen again.

My mother wept. She could not see her mother's body and could not perform a proper Buddhist cremation ritual. My mother believed her mother's ghost would remain in the world, alone, restlessly wandering the earth.

[lightening]

I tell my therapist that I have recently felt a sensation of *lightening*.

After a year of medical emergencies and hospitalizations, my son's medical condition has been diagnosed. I tell my therapist that I broke down and cried in the doctor's office when I got this news. The tears, blocked these days by my own new antidepressant medication, came flooding out of me like a wellspring. I had been holding on to the belief, for over two years, that my "defective" genes, poisoned by my family history, had flowed through me to my son. But I had been wrong. The unexpected test results had released something within me.

My therapist asks me if I mean *lightening* as in weight or as in electricity. *As in weight,* I say, *but now that I think about it, also as in a flash of light.* He says he pictures a weight being strapped to my ankle, dragging me down and immobilizing me. I wonder if it is possible to be paralyzed in one place and also moving everywhere, frantically, at the same time. The chaos and noise raging inside me drowns out everything all the time. He says sometimes a *rhyming* happens at different points in time, that the personal chaos within can match the spiral of violence without. *This rhyming doesn't always have to drag you down*, he says. It can generate new things.

He asks me to consider what I have drawn on to navigate the crisis of the past two years—in the university, in the medical system, in the home. I tell him: *I'm thinking of my father and my mother—all that they did to keep me alive.*

Your son's really lucky to have you as a mother, he says. *Lucky to have someone who has done so much to fight for his life.*

[fearless]

I'm eleven months old when my family resettles in the small town of Goderich, Ontario. My mother hears from her sister in Cambodia that the family has performed a Buddhist ceremony for their mother. My grandmother's remains are never found, but the family recovers a single photograph. Monks are called in and the customary rituals are performed. My aunt tells my mother not to be sad anymore, there have been enough tears for a lifetime.

Later in life, I would think repeatedly about my parents' ability to survive in those early years. How did they live each day knowing what they knew, what they had been through? I thought about how reinventing their lives in Canada required its own kind of *kamleang chet*, a kind that required abandoning the past so as to survive day by day. I thought about how it took almost thirty years before my mother was able to go back to Cambodia to make a Buddhist offering at her mother's shrine, and how happy she had been to come home after that trip.

Anida Yoeu Ali, Offerings, *from* The Buddhist Bug *series*
(Archival Inkjet Print, 2014). Photo by Vinh Dao. Courtesy of Studio Revolt.

Dearest Kai,

Happy third birthday Kai! You may always remember 2020 as the year a pandemic kept us all together, and brought you very close to your grandparents who have lived with us since January. For the year you've slept in our closet, which we converted into a bedroom for you. You also made a new friend—mousey, one of many mice who now run through our house searching for food! "Where is mousey?" you sometimes say.

This pandemic has given us time to bond, and to appreciate the home we live in. Being able to afford a home like this was your mama's dream come true. It may be a small condo with the occasional rodent, but it is safe, comfortable, and beautiful. When your mama was growing up, your grandparents did not have much money, so we lived in very modest homes or apartments. Your mama usually felt embarrassed or ashamed to invite her friends over because she remembered them making fun of the broken furniture, the yellow-stained walls, and the clutter that was everywhere. When mama was your age, she lived in a tattered old apartment in Goderich, Ontario, owned by the Church.

We lived under the townspeople's watchful eyes and never felt entirely comfortable.

In the past year, this new home has already given us so many joyful memories, laughter, movie nights, walks to the beach nearby, and parties and gatherings with our friends. When we were looking for a home, your father and I took you to many house showings around the area before we settled on this one. We knew this was the one right away because you seemed overjoyed running up and down the hallway entrance and around the front yard, eyes wide with excitement, saying wooooow, woooow.

Your grandparents have been such a gift to us during the lockdowns, even though we, at times, thought that living with five people in such a small place could drive us up the walls (it often did!). You became so connected with your grandparents that I sometimes got jealous that you'd rather play with them than me. Your auntie Maddie always said you had a wise soul, so it's no wonder that you talk to adults, and the older the better!

The pandemic has helped us forget about your health issues, the hospital visits, the fear and mourning that surrounded us. Before the pandemic, we lost your Uncle Don, someone irreplace-able in our lives. We took you to Ontario to see your grandparents and your uncles and cousin, while we went to our dear friend Don's memorial. He meant a great deal to me, and I feel a bit more alone in the world without him. He was there for me when I first went to graduate school, when I moved to Hong Kong, and he was there the night your father and I met. He held you once, played with you, and though his death was very sudden we are grateful for these memories.

You may not remember your Uncle Don well, but you will always see his picture in our living room. He was, and always will be, part of our home.

love always,
your mom
August 30, 2020

[nice]

One day, while following the threads of my family history for a school project, I come across a newspaper article in the Montreal *Gazette* dated December 4, 1980. I see the headline, "Snow Looks Nice to Asian Refugees," and below it an image of my mother and me. With this random unearthing, I feel a mixed sensation of warmth and detachment. I recognize something in my mother's expression, yet there is something out of alignment in the framing. From the past, the story of our arrival reaches out to me, touches me.

What catches my attention is my mother's unrestrained, radiant smile. I've seen my mother smiling in photos hundreds of times throughout my life, but I've never seen her smile captured this way. Is that the famous Cambodian smile? Is she conscious of the camera? After so much loss, can this photo be true? What can possibly be true and not true anymore after all that has happened?

In the photo, my mother's gaze is cast downward at me, a child of eleven months in her arms. Bundled in winter clothing, I look directly into the camera. The woolly winter hat I'm wearing forms the shape of an egg around my face. My mother wears the

Hello, Canada: Cheaung Yok Troeung with her 11-month-old baby Y Dang Troeung

The Montreal Gazette, *December 4, 1980.*

same kind of hat. We look so *cute and charming* in these Canadian clothes that have been collected for us in advance by our sponsors and the government. A small Canadian flag, my very first toy in this new land, peeks out from my coat. We are standing outside against the night sky. A light dusting of snow covers us. The image is serene, creating an impression of purity, innocence, and heroic motherhood.

The caption under the photo reads: "Hello, Canada: Cheaung Yok Troeung with her 11-month-old baby Y Dang Troeung." I notice my mother's maiden name and realize that this is the first time I've ever seen it spelled in English. Like Troeung, Cheaung (莊) is an uncommon transliteration of a Chinese surname, one that marks a transit through Cambodia.

But my mother's family, the Cheaung family, was almost entirely gone in 1980. Only one sister and one brother survived the genocide. In this photo she leaves them, and so many others, behind.

I read the text of the Montreal *Gazette* article and hold my breath: "The Cambodian baby waved a Canadian flag as the Troeung family set foot on Canadian soil—or rather snow—for the first time last night. It was a fitting start for the family of refugees about to start a new life in Goderich, Ontario . . . In high spirits after a gruelling 17-hour flight from Bangkok to Mirabel Airport, the Troeungs peered out at the white stuff on the ground and said: 'It looks nice—because it's different.'" As I read these lines, I think of snow as a symbol of Canada, Canada as the Great White North, *tabula rasa*. The story charms and delights. What could be more delightful than an account of snow looking nice to Asian refugees?

When I think of climate, I think about the war against nature that my parents faced just a year earlier. I picture them battered by the tropical elements, sleeping on the bare earth, exposed to the torrential monsoon rains and floods for nearly four years during the war. I see them foraging for food in the raging rivers, amidst wild animals. I'm haunted by the image of them walking for days, for weeks, through the jungle, through fields of landmines, through mountains parched dry by the burning hot sun, terrified of the earth itself.

In this story of arrival, however, it is the great Canadian climate that takes centre stage. It is an account of goodness, of *good refugees* entering the *good refuge*. It is a tale of refugees encountering a foreign, awe-inspiring land, an arc that forever fixes upon us the gaze of the sponsor and her land. In this story, we are "the lucky ones" who have survived with practically nothing, ready to become reborn.

I continue reading the *Gazette* article: "Clothes are all they packed in their suitcases; after a year in three different refugee camps it's all they have left. Baby Y Dang Troeung was born in a refugee camp in Thailand last January." I think of the clothes and styles that my mother has cast off many times in her past: her bell-bottoms and flower-print shirts, her sarongs and chi paos, discarded immediately in the rush of April 17, 1975; the revolutionary attire of Democratic Kampuchea, thrown off and burned after January 7, 1979; the salvaged apparel of the old days traded in at the border camps for the donated garb arriving off the trucks.

The story of arrival tells of the piles of things that will be awaiting my family in our new rural home, things that will make us more Canadian with each passing year. In Goderich, among our sponsors—those kind and not-so-kind souls who will come and go over the years—we will learn a new language, take on a new religion, and learn to let the past go. Survival in Canada's harsh winter climate will require a blanketing of all that came before.

I look back at the smile on my mother's face. Only thirty-three years old in this photo, she had lived so many lives already. Here she is crossing into a new life, a new start. Yet there is something true captured in her smile, something cracking through the frame, something the story of arrival leaves to the snow and the wind.

Plans had been made to welcome the symbolic final refugees: two Cambodian brothers and their families—four adults and six children—destined to a Mennonite congregation in Goderich, Ontario. A day or two after arrival, the family was whisked off to Parliament Hill, where they were formally welcomed by Prime Minister Trudeau and Minister Axworthy. Everyone smiled. The cameras clicked.

—Michael J. Molloy et al., *Running on Empty:
Canada and the Indochinese Refugees, 1975–1980*

Prime Minister Pierre Trudeau welcoming my family to Canada, December 1980. Courtesy of the Troeung family.

[sampeah]

It's 2015. I come across a video in the CBC archives titled "Pierre Elliott Trudeau welcomes Cambodian refugees in 1980." I know this scene of arrival well. I have fragments of this scene at home with me in the form of a photo album commemorating the event: we were the "last" of the sixty thousand refugees sponsored by Canada under the Canadian government's special "Indochinese Refugee Program." Given to us by the Canadian government in 1980, this album has travelled far: from Ottawa, to Goderich, to Cambridge, to Hong Kong, to an exhibit at the Royal Ontario Museum in Toronto, to Vancouver. Over the years, other photos and newspaper clippings have been added to the album: some photos taken in Khao-I-Dang, as well as newspaper stories from the Montreal *Gazette*, the *Goderich Signal Star*, and CBC News.

There is one photo in the album that I refer to as *the* photo of arrival. I am all the way at the back, a baby in my mother's arms. Alongside my mother stands my father, my aunt, uncle, and cousins. They face Prime Minister Pierre Elliott Trudeau and Immigration Minister Lloyd Axworthy. Trudeau holds up his two hands, palms facing together, in the traditional Cambodian gesture known as the *sampeah*. Deriving from Khmer Buddhism, the sampeah is a Buddhist form of respectful greeting, as well as a common way to express gratitude or apology. I wonder: Who is being respectful or polite in this scene? Who is grateful or apologetic?

My father remembers the days and hours leading up to the scene captured in the photo: the long flight from Thailand to Montreal on a Boeing 747 filled with Cambodian and Laotian refugees; the blistering cold weather of the Montreal airport tarmac; the rush to outfit all the refugees with winter coats, hats, and boots; the boots that my two brothers wore on the wrong feet for days afterwards; the military base in Montreal used to temporarily warehouse the planeload of refugees; the lineups for food (eggs, beans, corn, apples, bananas) at the military base; the Canadian people standing behind the buffet line serving food.

One by one, the sponsors arrive at the military camp to pick up their refugee families. One day, all the other refugees are gone and only my family remains. No one speaks Khmer. No one has tried to speak Chinese. My father has no way to ask why our sponsors haven't come. Everyone communicates entirely through body language. At last, two big Canadian men arrive and escort my family to a bus that takes us to Ottawa. They put us in a hotel until our sponsors arrive. The sponsors are not a single family, but a group of seven adults. One is a priest. He draws a picture on a piece of paper telling my father it is time to go downstairs to eat. My father only knows one phrase in English—*Thank you*.

The next day we arrive at the Parliament Buildings in Ottawa and meet a Cambodian interpreter who says to my father in Khmer, *Your family is so lucky. Important people from a small town have sponsored you.* He uses the words *anak mean*, people who have means.

My family is escorted to an observation room where they can see a Parliament session in action. We are shuttled to a room reserved for tea at Parliament Hill. Here, the interpreter says to my father: *You will now meet the prime minister and immigration minister to say thank you to Canada. I will interpret for you.* The moment arrives and my father says in Khmer: *I represent my family and my brother's family. Thank you for opening the door to let us come to have a new life.* He is surprised that the prime minister knows how to perform the gesture of the sampeah. They bow to each other, and the prime minister makes his way down the line.

Throughout my life, I have wondered if the smiles and sampeahs in this photo of arrival held a deeper pain, the pain of losing a country, the hurt of leaving people behind, the heartache of smiling in the wake of death.

[duty]

My parents named me after the refugee camp Khao-I-Dang not just to remember their survival, but to honour the international aid workers who cared for them after an improbable escape from the labour camps in Cambodia, across the landmine-riddled jungle, to the border of Thailand. As difficult and confusing as my name is, I wonder now how my life would have turned out had they instead named me "Goderich," after the small Canadian town where a kind group of sponsors pooled their resources to bring us to Canada. Or if they had named me "Trudeau," after the man who greeted me as an infant when my family first arrived in Canada, the man who is the centrepiece of my family's postcard-perfect photograph commemorating our arrival.

The scholar Sara Ahmed speaks of the "Happiness Duty" of the migrant, which means "telling a certain story about your arrival as good, or the good of your arrival." With my family living in poverty, and haunted by the knowledge of those left behind, I had difficulty performing this duty. I remember reliving my family's experience as a child. I remember the words thrown my way. "Genocide" was not an accurate definition of what happened, I was told. That term must be reserved for the *real* genocides. "Death" was too heavy for a child to say. But I could say "tragedy." I could talk about how terrible war was. War in the abstract, as if what happened to us was an abstract thing.

The resurgence of private sponsorship reflected the strong advocacy of Cambodian groups to encourage private sponsors to resettle their friends and relatives. Church sponsors worked with one another to help reunite Cambodians. St. Peter's Catholic Church in Goderich sponsored two brothers and their families in December 1980. They invited a third brother and sister with her accompanying family, who had been sponsored by the town's Knox Presbyterian Church in March 1980, to live together in a former convent that had been renovated by members of St. Peter's congregation.

—Janet McLellan, *Cambodian Refugees in Ontario: Resettlement, Religion, and Identity*

[showpiece]

It is the fall of 2015. From Hong Kong, I am watching the Syrian refugee crisis unfold by the day on the news. It is crushing and surreal to watch. I receive a message from my friend Vinh in Toronto who asks me to contribute an essay for the website Compassionate Canada, a collection of testimonials by former Southeast Asian refugees in solidarity with Syrian refugees. The rationale is as follows: "If a narrative of Canada's compassion toward Southeast Asian refugees was going to be celebrated, then we wanted to utilize this public celebration to advocate for those currently in dire need of assistance. We wanted the opportunity to tell our stories, and to determine how these stories get used politically—to stand in support of, and solidarity with, millions of displaced people."

At first, I'm reluctant. I dislike drawing attention to myself, and my time in Hong Kong, since becoming one of the youngest professors to win my university's Teaching Excellence Award, has cast a relentless spotlight on me. For six months, I have been bombarded with the same image of my own smiling face as I hold up the award placard. This image has greeted me on the university's webpage, in every classroom I teach in, and on the subway walls, where my parents have posed with it to create their own image.

All this attention has exhausted and depleted me. I have the constant impulse to hide myself away, to disappear forever into the anonymity of Phnom Penh, but something always calls me back to the world. The scenes of death, boats, bodies, and separations repeat night after night, a ceaseless volume and noise. How many times can I tell my story? Somehow I muster the energy, tamp down the embarrassment, and write a short one-page piece, entitled "Never a Last Refugee."

Months later, my friend posts the essay on Compassionate Canada. I watch from Hong Kong as the essay circulates online. Comments and shares begin to accumulate. I scan the comments below the essay while partly shielding my eyes from the screen, as if my hands will help me filter out unwanted incomings. One comment from copd4real beckons me with that infamous phrase, *if you don't mind my asking*:

> Thank you for sharing such a mixed story of blessings and bureaucratic indifference to the lives the numbers represent. If you don't mind my asking, did you move to Hong Kong to be closer to a prosperous culture that looks like you, or to escape the status of "showpiece" in a white-bred, possibly Xenophobic adopted country? There are such nuances of hope and loss within your tale, that I'd love to learn more about your tale. Thank you for writing such a timely piece.

I chuckle at copd4real's querying. Showing him the comment, I say to my partner, Chris, *actually I think I am tired of being a "showpiece,"* of being the object in every commemoration, exhibition, special-issue cover, history book, academic article, and news story produced and reproduced by everyone but myself.

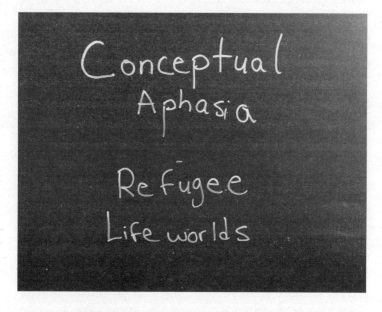

An early chalkboard brainstorm for what would eventually become my first book, Refugee Lifeworlds.

[slow]

How many times have I come across a fragment in a book about Canadian history and wondered if I would ever find the level of stability of body and mind required to write my family's own story?

I have for many years marvelled at the speed at which non-Cambodian scholars can generate and publish their accounts of Cambodian history, sometimes even embedding my family's story somewhere within their articles and books. I think of the Cambodian American poet Monica Sok, who writes about the drafts and drafts of her poetry she tears up, paralyzed by the fear of misrepresenting her family's history. Like her, I feel that my slow, excruciating writing process is both my greatest strength and my curse. Will I be forever relegated to the object of my own story? Or should I just feel grateful to have such a powerful account to share?

Many have reminded me over the years that the coincidence of my history has granted me a position that they (non-Cambodians) only wish they could have. Being a showpiece, an inspiration for others, a poster child for the Canadian state, some have implied, has come with some benefits. I have a Ph.D. in literature. I am a scholar at one of the top institutions in Canada, working on Cambodian refugee history. And yet, I am paralyzed when it comes to writing my own story.

There are so few scholarly, research-driven books about Cambodian experience authored by Cambodian refugees themselves. So few Cambodian refugees are in academic positions in the first place, and so few are willing to take on the burden of expectation, the life-engulfing experience of being thrust into the spotlight. If we fail, we fail not just ourselves, but our entire history.

I long to write my story in a way that shows the cracks and fissures beneath the refugee's smile of gratitude. At the same time, I cannot deny that, for the kindness shown to my family, for the opportunities to research and learn and perhaps one day write, I am and continue to be grateful, *genuinely* grateful.

Struck between the smooth surfaces and the burrowed fissures, I am again stuck.

[viewings]

In 2017, we are asked to lend our family photos to the Royal Ontario Museum for an exhibition entitled *The Family Camera* that is held to coincide with the commemoration of Canada's 150th anniversary. One of our photographs is exhibited in a section thematically focused on intersections between family photography and Canadian national history.

I wonder how the viewing audience of the museum's white space will interpret the smiles of my mother and father shown in the photo taken with Pierre Trudeau. Will they see grateful refugees, or will they see cynical performances of gratitude that mask a deeper resentment? How can anyone begin to interpret the expressed emotions of refugees, whose feelings are submerged in unimaginable loss and years of catastrophic upheaval?

Today, I keep this photograph with Pierre Trudeau in a family album in my bedroom cabinet, while my aunt and uncle in Toronto have theirs framed and hanging in their living room. Over forty years later, they are still proud to have this photograph.

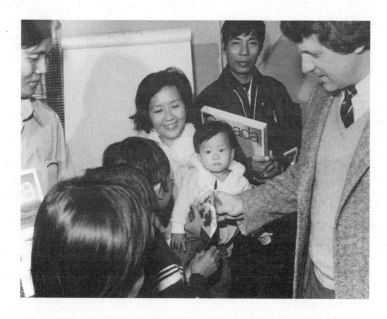

Welcome ceremony at Parliament Hill with Immigration Minister
Lloyd Axworthy, December 1980. Courtesy of the Troeung family.

[the word]

What does the word *refugee* do for us? We, who have been named and disciplined by this word? We who have felt this word foisted upon us, shaping and directing our routes and trajectories, our legibility, creating the parameters of what is permissible or impermissible for us to speak?

A refugee exists within a continuum of the displaced. Asylum seekers, migrants, undocumented persons. The boundaries among these categories are porous. A subject in extra-territorial limbo, the refugee exists within a field of administrative power. They negotiate with state laws, institutions, charities, and agencies.

As a person who belongs to no nation, the refugee plays a role in the new nation's self-exaltation. The term is often deployed to the detriment of other minority groups, the undeserving poor in opposition to the poor deserving Asian refugee. I have witnessed firsthand the Canadian state's adulation of my own refugee image, only so others can cast me as someone stuck in my own victimization.

What remains in the hearts, minds, bodies of survivors exceeds the state's ability for meaningful redress. It exceeds the laws of justice itself. Here, in the space of loss and survival, injury and joy, the refugee makes and remakes life, confronts death, and grapples with the difficulty of language and meaning in the afterlife.

[commemoration]

It's December 2019. A reporter from the CBC in Vancouver contacts me for an interview. They want to do the interview in my home. They want me to talk about my photos with Pierre Trudeau. Here's the story: *It's the fortieth anniversary of Canada's private refugee sponsorship program and your family's arrival in Canada. What happened after your family's arrival? How do you feel today? I'm assuming, proud to be Canadian?*

At the interview, the reporter tells me to talk *like a human being, not a professor.* She seems to be trying to trick me into revealing my parents' *true age.*

I watch the CBC's fortieth-anniversary commemoration of my family's arrival on television. There I am again. There, that same image of me as a baby waving the Canadian flag flashing across the screen. Why did I do this? Who is my story inspiring? Inspiring them to do what?

In 2021, I write to the CBC asking them to take down the photos of me and my family published in their 2019 human interest story, "'The wounds never go away': Baby Y-Dang named after Cambodian refugee camp remembers Canadian arrival." I tell

My father and I being welcomed to Canada.

them that, because I was experiencing deep distress and anxiety, I did not understand that those photographs would remain on the CBC's website indefinitely. The CBC journalist says she saw no evidence that I was experiencing a mental health crisis at the time of the interview. They deny my request. The commemoration lives on.

[swirl]

I do not call myself a refugee poster child as a cynical recollec-tion. In 2018, I went from being designated the "last" refugee of Canada to becoming the first Southeast Asian refugee to work in the University of British Columbia's English department, perhaps the first in all of the arts faculty. The question I am always asked is never *are you grateful?* but *how grateful are you?*

Of course anyone in my position would rather be "saved" than left behind to die in a genocide or refugee camp. Of course anyone would prefer to keep living, even if that meant seeing themselves cast as an inspiration, as a model of determination, as a minor anec-dote in the story of Canadian exceptionalism, even if it exhausted them every time they saw it.

I am not the only poster child. There is a long history of parad-ing disabled children as poster children for medical and scientific fundraising. I survived, but I am persistently angry that my image is casually used to sanitize and deflect from the suffering of other peoples in Canada and in the world.

Like many refugee stories before mine, I know mine will be seen through the analytical prisms of suspicion from all sides of the

Black Hole, *drawn by hand with black ink pen (2020).*
Artwork by Visothkakvei. Courtesy of the artist.

political spectrum. I know I may be dismissed as a non-authority by some, or as a sellout by others. I know writing my story may take more from me than it will ever give back, because it will mean dwelling in a vacuum of silence, self-doubt, and isolation. Sometimes, writing my story will be like wandering inside, around, and through my own madness. It is this mad act that draws me into that dark, swirling place, from which I may never escape.

[first and last]

In 2015, I watch a news video of recently elected Canadian prime minister Justin Trudeau welcoming the first planeload of Syrian refugees to Canada. These refugees are being commemorated as the *first flight in a government program to resettle Syrians in Canada.* To the camera, Trudeau explains that the welcome ceremony is an attempt *to show the world how to open our hearts and welcome in people who are fleeing extraordinarily difficult situations. . . . They step off the plane as refugees, but they walk out of this terminal as permanent residents of Canada.* Trudeau shakes hands with Syrian men and women as they disembark from the plane; he presents a young child with a new winter coat; he reaches out to touch the arm of an infant held in her father's arms.

The gesture of welcome echoes across time and space. I am taken back to the CBC video of my family in 1980, where Pierre Trudeau reaches out to pat my infant head. I see the uncanny reflection between the Syrian girl and the Cambodian girl, the First and the Last showpieces in the nation's reiterating master-narrative of benevolence. I see the mirroring of the current Trudeau and his father, figures of national magnanimity. Good men, good refuge,

Canadian prime minister Justin Trudeau welcomes first planeload of government-sponsored Syrian refugees, 2015.

From the CBC archives: "Former Canadian prime minister Pierre Elliott Trudeau welcomes a family of Cambodian refugees in 1980."

good refugee. I see the online comments below the "welcome" videos, full of vitriol and hate directed at both groups of refugees. Forty years apart, the Syrian girl and the Cambodian girl are part of the same image repertoire. I want that silent, wide-eyed child at the back of the photo of arrival to speak. I want to speak to that child and tell her that I'll find a way to tell her story, with love and dignity, on her own terms, when the time comes.

Dearest Kai,

On your fourth birthday, most of your gifts have consisted of number games, which you absorb and make your own. You invent rules for new games to play with little number tiles, and you are clearly gifted at math. You've gone from an interest in addition and subtraction to understanding multiplication, division, fractions, and algebra. Sometimes you carry calculators with you everywhere, even to the potty, and whenever we leave the house you always bring at least one of your three watches!

Earlier this year, we came to better understand your neurodiversity, and in turn, we began to realize the ways that your father and I have always operated differently from those around us. Learning this made us love you all the more! We love all the things that make you you, because you remind us of our love for each other. You're the most fun-loving, gentle, and caring spirit we've ever encountered.

You are getting older, but you still love me and want to cuddle and kiss me. I dread the day you are too old for this! So, for now I enjoy it as much as I can. My love for you has been different from the love I've felt for anyone. I don't know what to do with the intense feelings of love and joy I have when holding you, when seeing you giggle, when watching you play with numbers or with the educators at daycare. It has felt like a serene joy mixed with an intense panic. In the same moment of pride, I feel shaken and reduced. What does it mean to love someone so helpless, but who, day by day, needs you less and less?

Today you are turning four. You are healthy now, though I often forget you are no longer weak. I still cannot enter the Children's Hospital for your checkups. I still feel panic when you go to sleep. But I believe that this panic no longer comes from being afraid something will happen to you, but because every moment seems so fleeting. You will smile or cry and then the moment will be gone, never to be seen again.

In the future, as you grow older, I will mourn these moments even more.

love always,
your mom
August 30, 2021

[return]

After the war, my mother had hoped she would hear from her brother in Russia. She believed he had been spared the suffering since he had been working abroad when the Khmer Rouge came to power. After years passed, without any news from him, my mother began to fear the worst.

My mother tells me this story again in 2008. For about a year, I have been recording my parents' oral histories in earnest. Listening to their stories about Cambodia has become a new obsession for me, and I record over twenty hours of their testimony. As a part of my work, I am making a radio documentary for the CBC. I pitch them several titles. They settle on "The Lucky One Returns."

Here's the story: After thirty years, you go back to Cambodia with your mother to help her find out what happened to her brother who disappeared.

It is my second time in Cambodia since my first visit in 2005, and my mother's first time since the end of the war. I bring my mother to the infamous Tuol Sleng Genocide Museum in Phnom Penh. The space is visceral and shocking to take in. We scan the museum displays for a mug shot photo of my mother's brother, now rumoured to have been transferred to Tuol Sleng during Pol Pot time. Over the next decade I will return to Tuol Sleng many, many times.

I feel jolted out of all my romanticized illusions of return. The trip has been hard on my mother. She has wanted so badly to help me with my documentary, has spent hours reliving the past for my recorder, but at what cost? In my obsession to tell her story, I thought only of reunion, catharsis, recovery. Now, here we are, confronted by horrors we're unprepared for. I'm disoriented and need to walk the streets to get some air.

In his last letters to my mother, my uncle wrote that one day he would return to Cambodia from Moscow. He had been living in Moscow for fourteen years, first as a foreign student studying architectural engineering and then as a diplomat at the Cambodian embassy in Moscow, working for Prince Norodom Sihanouk and preparing to be the next Cambodian ambassador in France. My uncle wrote to tell my mother that he was in love with a woman from Ukraine, that he had fathered two children with this woman. They had created a family together in Moscow.

At Tuol Sleng, my mother and I search the compound for hours, looking for my uncle's picture. She stops frequently to explain things to me, and identifies some of the people in the archival photos on display. *Look, that's Pol Pot, Ieng Sary, and Nuon Chea. You see, this is what they did. Can you believe this?* We see the torture instruments on display, the floors stained red. We hear the ghost stories: in the years after Pol Pot time, the juice of the coconut trees around Tuol Sleng turned sour.

The high-pitched sound of screams could be heard at night. Eventually we give up searching for my uncle's photo, but we notice that there is a documentation archive adjacent to the museum space. We go there and ask the archivist if she can help us. The archivist searches through several files looking for my uncle's name but finds nothing.

We almost give up, but then my mother mentions that my uncle was a foreign student studying in Russia before the war. The archivist goes immediately to retrieve another file. She gives us a thin book with a cover image showing a shirtless, emaciated man in a prison cell, his foot shackled to the wall.

I would later discover that this image was a drawing by Vann Nath, the first survivor of the prison to write a memoir of his time there, *A Cambodian Prison Portrait: One Year in the Khmer Rouge's S-21*. I would spend months after this trip writing an article about this book, absorbing time and again its visceral details of torture, unaware of the toll that this research could—and one day would—take upon me.

The archivist tells us that this book is the record of the foreign students and diplomats who were transferred to Tuol Sleng. The book is in a deteriorating condition, its pages yellowing and coming apart at the seams. My mother goes through each page slowly, running her finger down the list of names. She gets to page fifty-three and cries out in recognition when she sees her brother's name.

The archivist takes out a pink highlighter and highlights my uncle's name and information. My mother's face becomes distant as she tries to translate the information for me. She tells me that my uncle entered Tuol Sleng on October 23, 1976, and died on

October 29, 1976. She repeats to me several times that he was only in this place for six days, as if she is telling this to herself. She reads the line listing her brother's cause of death and translates this for me. *Illness. He died of illness*. She seems to let out a sigh of relief but then notices that she has misread the information. *No, torture. It was torture*.

ល.រ	នាម និង នាមត្រកូល	ចាប់មកពី	មុខងារ	ថ្ងៃចាប់	ថ្ងៃកំទេច
1	រមៅ កូនហ្វុន្ធិ	ស្រុកបារាំង	និស្សិត	31-8-76	16-9-76
2	មៅ សួងប៉ុជា (ស្រី)	—	អគ្គលេខាឯងឧទនាគារ	1-9-76	16-9-76
3	ហ្ញត សំបាត់	—	ទូតប្រចាំប្រទេសយួហ្សោស្លាវី ឈ័ស្លាប់	9-9-76	17-11-76
4	ភ្ញុ ស៊ុបគន្ធី	—	ទូតប្រចាំស៊ុយអែដ	9-9-76	6-12-76
5	គុយ ជា	រស៊ុ	និយាយវិទ្យុស្ស	23-9-76	6-12-76
6	ភ្ញក សួរុត	បារាំង	អង្គការសហប្រជាជាតិ	23-9-76	6-12-76
7	ស្រ្ជ គឹមហួយ (ស្រី)	—	គ្រូបង្រៀន	23-9-76	6-12-76
8	ហ៊ីង សុខម	អាមេរិក	សាស្រ្តាចារ្យ	23-9-76	6-12-76
9	អ៊ុង រាត់ឃ័រ (ស្រី)	បារាំង	រដ្ឋបណ្ឌិត	23-9-76	6-12-76
10	ម៉ែន មុនីម៉ាម	—	—	12-10-76	18-3-77
11	ឧ្យង ឡេងឆេក	—	ប្រធានពោធចក្រុស្រាយ	12-10-76	6-12-76
12	ផ្ន សុវណ្ណហាន	—	និស្សិតខ្យាសាស្ត្រ	12-10-76	28-1-77
13	ហេង សុធហ្	—	និស្សិតគណិតវិទ្យា	12-10-76	28-1-77
14	ឡូវ វ៉ា	រស៊ុ	វិស្វករទិចប៉ិក	12-10-76	18-3-77
15	មៀច សួន	បារាំង	និស្សិតអគ្គិសនី	12-10-76	18-2-77
16	ថវង សេងណុង	—	សាស្រ្តាចារ្យ	12-10-76	21-12-76
17	ណឹម សុជិត	កាណាដា	និស្សិត	12-10-76	28-1-77
18	យ៉េប សុកធា	អាល់ហ្សេរី	សែតសំណាង់	12-10-76	6-12-76
19	រិន សុភ័ណ (ស្រី)	—	ប្រពន្ធយ៉េប សុកធា	12-10-76	6-12-76
20	ជីង កុកហ្ន	បារាំង	ភារ:ស្ទូមីស្ថានទូត « ស្លាប់ក្រី »	23-10-76	29-10-76
21	ភ្ញុ សេនាវី	—	និស្សិតកំចាញ	23-10-76	28-1-77
22	គ្ គឹមស្រី	—	និស្សិតពេទ្យ	23-10-76	18-3-77
23	នា គឹមស្រ៊ាង	—	និហារណី នាហារណី	23-10-76	18-3-77
24	ហេង ស៊ុហេៀង(ស្រី)	—	ប្រពន្ធនាគឹមស្រ៊ាង	23-10-76	28-1-77
25	ឡ្យាយ រ៉ុល	—	និស្សិតអគ្គិសនី	23-10-76	28-1-77
26	ភ្ញុ ឡូវ	—	ព្រសួងផែនការ	23-10-76	18-2-77

In highlighting, my uncle's name ជីង កុកហ្ន *(Ching "Cheung" Kok Hour)*
and association បារាំង *(France), occupation* ភារ:ស្ទូមីស្ថានទូត
(ambassador), and his reason for death "ស្លាប់ក្រី" *(literally, "die poor").*
From the Tuol Sleng Genocide Museum.

[pray]

While my mother and I are in Phnom Penh piecing together the
story of my uncle's disappearance, the trial for Kaing Guek Eav,
the former Khmer Rouge leader in charge of S-21, has just begun.
My mother follows the news of the tribunal as it unfolds, but she
seems ambivalent about it overall. I ask her if she wants to attend
the trial, which could be one of the most significant events in modern Cambodian history, and one of the most important human
rights trials of all time. She decides no, she would rather spend our
time left with her sister in Phnom Penh.

We attend a family wedding, a joyous celebration and a full day
of rituals. We watch a red knot–tying ceremony—the blessing and
binding of two souls and families together. I never intend to marry
anyone, I think, but someday I would like to have a red knot ceremony, to bind my soul with someone I love.

My mother takes me to her hometown in Kampong Thom and
shows me her childhood home and the building that used to be a
cinema run by her father. Together, we burn incense in front of
the Buddhist shrine to honour the dead.

If you don't truly believe, she tells me, *just don't go in. You have to
pray with honesty in your heart.*

[disappeared]

Years after my mother and I visit Tuol Sleng, we are able to piece together some of the missing fragments of my uncle's story. The Documentation Center of Cambodia, or DC-Cam, helps us retrieve my uncle's prison biography and S-21 mug shot. My mother hardly recognizes her brother in the photo. It is him, and yet is not him. He looks so different from the way she remembers him. Could these cold, vacant eyes be those of her beloved brother? She notices that his name is also recorded differently in this file. His biography is so sparse, and some details do not make sense. The researchers at DC-Cam tell me his case seems highly unusual.

My uncle had been working as *chargé d'affaires* at the Cambodian embassy in France during the reign of Norodom Sihanouk. In exile in China, Sihanouk had called for a regathering of all the Khmer intellectuals dispersed in Cambodia's Cold War networks abroad. The civil war with Lon Nol had come to an end, Sihanouk said, and it was time for all patriotic Cambodians to return to Democratic Kampuchea to help *rebuild the country*. They would be welcomed by the Khmer Rouge. The delegation of Sihanouk's government in exile landed at Pochentong Airport in 1975.

Sihanouk was put under house arrest while the rest of the delegation, including my uncle, were disappeared and never seen again.

To disappear in Pol Pot time meant getting lost to vast networks of torture, death, and unmarked graves. As the Cambodian countryside was restructured into labour co-operatives where people were starved, worked to the point of exhaustion, and left to die, the Khmer Rouge established over three hundred sites of direct killing. The most infamous among these was S-21, a converted urban high school known as Tuol Sleng, and Choeung Ek, a former Chinese cemetery. At Tuol Sleng S-21 Security Center, prisoners were subject to a wide array of brutal interrogation methods designed to uncover their perceived ties to the enemies of the regime such as the Vietnamese government, CIA, or KGB. An estimated 14,000 to 20,000 people were murdered at Tuol Sleng, with only a small number of inmates surviving their incarceration. The dead speak to the extreme paranoia that undergirded Pol Pot's revolution, as the majority of people killed at Tuol Sleng, especially in the later part of the revolution, were former Khmer Rouge cadres themselves. The school-turned-prison exhibits the blurred distinctions between victims and perpetrators.

Initially, those executed at Tuol Sleng were taken to urban areas adjacent to the prison for burial in mass graves. As this practice became unsustainable for the regime, prisoners were transferred to Choeung Ek, also known as "the Killing Fields," an area about seventeen kilometres south of Phnom Penh, where they were beaten to death by blunt force trauma to the head, their bodies thrown into mass graves of up to 450 people and dissolved by the chemical DDT to suppress the smell.

At Choeung Ek, as many as three hundred prisoners were killed in a day, and after 1979, it was revealed that the site's 2.4 hectares of land consisted of 129 mass graves containing the remains of twenty thousand victims. Today, these remains are housed in a large Buddhist memorial stupa and cared for by local keepers. Visited by tourists and Cambodians alike, the memorials at Tuol Sleng and Choeung Ek serve as *documentation for all of mankind* of the *dreadful things that happened from '75 to '79.*

Tuol Sleng, 2005. Photograph by Y-Dang Troeung.

[shot]

The activities at Tuol Sleng involved the compilation of thousands of prisoner dossiers, including mug shots, prisoner biographies, autobiographical confessions, and interrogation notes.

The file of Hout Bophana, sometimes referred to today as *the Anne Frank of Cambodia*, continues to stand as one of the most complete of these dossiers. Hout Bophana's S-21 archive has drawn the attention of many for its detailed portrait of a Cambodian woman who wrote love letters to her husband from S-21 alongside thousands of pages of false confessions.

The defiant gaze that emanates from Hout Bophana's S-21 mug shot has been a source of inspiration for many Cambodian films and artistic works. It is an image that has become emblematic of Cambodian people's quiet forms of rebellion and resistance during Pol Pot time, and inspired the creation of the Bophana Audiovisual Resource Center in Phnom Penh, established by the filmmaker Rithy Panh to document and preserve Cambodian history.

In April 2021, I cannot stop thinking about Hout Bophana's image when I am told by many friends, simultaneously, that the Tuol Sleng mug shots are igniting controversy again. The US media group *VICE* has published an article featuring mug shots that have been colourized and digitally altered to show victims at Tuol Sleng *smiling*. I cannot look at them, but I imagine the smile, the Cambodian smile, famous for warming tourists with its child-like innocence. Somehow, the person who altered these photos says he is doing so to humanize the victims.

I am out-of-body, unable to conceive how any news outlet could reproduce these images and call it *humanity*. I ask someone to look through the images for me, paranoid that my uncle might be among the altered. Thankfully, he is not.

I sign petitions, but I'm too frozen in disbelief to do more. Soon enough, so many Cambodian people decry the indignity that *VICE* removes the article.

I think of Hout Bophana's defiant gaze and wonder how anyone could see her image and believe it wasn't already human. I find myself unravelling. Why the smile? Why is it *always* about the smile? For whom would a Cambodian victim of torture and death not be human, except when smiling?

[smile]

Refugees are made to smile; perhaps we would not be human otherwise. For us, the smile is not an expression of happiness, but a shape bent and tweaked by the people around us. Our smile is the clothing we present to an icy world; it is how we shield ourselves from cold. Though the smile may stiffen into place, it never feels natural.

Trained in the arts of performance, we suspect the smiles of others, fearful that behind every smile is another person who wants to destroy us. Paranoia floats above every encounter, every outing.

The smile brings exhaustion. Sometimes, our anger broaches the armour of the smile—the anger that builds with every daily diminishment, cracking our smiles with small tremors. We fear that if our smiles break, the ghosts of our past will return.

The smile is the price of first-world admission. The smile makes us exceptional rather than ordinary, lucky rather than cursed. The smile makes us both the centre of attention and completely invisible.

I begin to see how a white photographer working for *VICE*, when encountering the defiant and angered faces of the Tuol Sleng victims, would feel the need to forcibly change them (the family's permissions be damned!). What is a Cambodian refugee without their smile? Who are we without the psychological breakdown that the demand for our smiles has wrought upon us?

Meant to invite one's gaze, the smile does not just portray gratitude. It searches, it sees, it guards. Those who believe in the smile, those who cannot see through it, can never know us.

In November 2021, my friends Colin and Keiko assist the Tuol Sleng Genocide Museum in constructing an online memorial to the victims of the Khmer Rouge, and ask me to provide information about my uncle. The archive assembles many years of research from a large network of historians and archivists. The memorial will have my uncle's mug shot, unaltered. It will have his biography alongside words from my mother about his life. I hope others will see it, that perhaps my uncle's wife and children, who have been lost to us, will one day see it and will use it to come and find their cousins.

When Colin and Keiko send me the final copy of my uncle's memorial, I am alone in my room, crying, and smiling too. I feel my uncle with me, the niece he never met. We smile together, and marvel at each other's beautiful faces.

[app]

Factsheet on Mr. Ching Kok Hour from the
Tuol Sleng Genocide Museum: "Life Stories of S-21 Prisoners"

PRISONER GROUP: RETURNEES

CHING KOK HOUR

Born into a Chinese family, he was multilingual and a student of
architecture in Russia, and probably left his family in Russia.

Date of birth: 1939 (approximate year of birth)

Place of birth: Kampong Thom

Father: died of illness before the war

Mother: died during Pol Pot time (body never located)

Siblings: five brothers, two sisters

He seemed to have a wife or partner (probably Ukrainian)
and two children

Date of arrest: 23 October 1976

Date of death: 29 October 1976

BEFORE COMING BACK FROM FRANCE TO CAMBODIA IN 1976
Ching Kok Hour's father was born in China, and his mother was born in Cambodia to a Chinese father and Cambodian mother. He was the eldest son and had five brothers and two sisters.

He went to a Chinese High School in Phnom Penh, and when he was 21 years old (probably in 1960), he went to Moscow, Russia.

Eang Saiha (one of his fellow students in Russia and also a victim of S-21) mentioned in his forced confession that he met Ching Kok Hour in 1962 in Russia.

Ching Kok Hour's name also appears on a report from Phnom Penh in French. The writer criticized students abroad, especially in Russia, who got into Marxism. He was listed as a "student won over by foreign ideology."

According to another victim's forced confession, Ching Kok Hour was in Beijing in 1972. Tep Sam An, who was sent to China as the third secretary of the Cambodian Embassy in China, wrote in his confession that he met Ching Kok Hour, who was the second secretary.

According to an interview with Ching Kok Hour's younger sister Yok Troeung via e-mail:

> "When my brother went to Russia, he went as a student to study architecture, then he became an engineer. Before 1975, I received a letter from him telling me that the Cambodian

government had offered him a job teaching engineering in the Russian school in Phnom Penh. My father did not approve of him coming back, so he stayed in Russia. He also wrote in the letter that when he came back to Cambodia, he would build a new, beautiful house for me. I also remember that the letter included a photo of him, wearing a Russian winter hat, with a Ukrainian woman who had short curly hair, a round face, and big eyes, and two small children (around one and two years old).

"He was really interested in politics and government. He was very handsome and also very intelligent. In Cambodia, he spoke Khmer and Fujian at home. When he went to school, he studied Guo-yi (Mandarin). He also had a private English tutor. As far as I remember, he didn't have any interest in communism or sports.

"The last time I heard from him, he was still in Russia and he was working as an engineer. In addition to Khmer, Chinese and English, he had learned to speak Russian, Spanish, French, and another two languages (unknown). I remember being impressed that he could speak eight different languages in total."

SUMMARY OF DOCUMENTS FOUND AT TUOL SLENG
GENOCIDE MUSEUM

There are at least six lists mentioning his name. According to them, he was already sick when he was sent to S-21 and he died before the interrogation so that there is no confession. He was listed as "an acting ambassador" on some documents but there is no mention of which embassy. He was listed as "(came back) from France"; however, the museum doesn't know when he came back.

Ching Kok Hour's sister survived and arrived in Khao I Dang (Cambodian refugee camp near the Thai border) in 1979, then moved to Canada in 1981. Around 1983, someone in Cambodia informed her that they had seen her brother's photo on display at S-21.

Ching Kok Hour's sister and her daughter, Y-Dang Troeung, found out that he died at S-21 in 1976, when they visited Tuol Sleng Genocide Museum in 2008. They were given the booklet of a list of prisoners that includes "Returnees." The main reason that Y-Dang Troeung was looking for her uncle's information was "trying to locate his children in Russia. Presumably, they have never known what happened to their father after he returned to Cambodia in 1976." As far as Ching Kok Hour's sister knows, he never went to France from Russia. She was surprised to learn from his S-21 file that he had anything to do with the Cambodian embassy in France. She was never in contact with the family in Russia. She often wonders if they are still alive today. The family doesn't have any photos of him. Only his two sisters and one brother are known to be alive. The museum found a photo taken at S-21, and his name in the articles and other prisoners' confessions. The museum team made contact with Y-Dang, who interviewed her mother for this research.

00754

Ching "Cheung" Kok Hour's photo at S-21 (© Tuol Sleng Genocide Museum).
Courtesy of the Museum.

Dearest Kai,

I am writing this sooner than I thought. I am writing this from St. Paul's Hospital, and I am writing now because I am afraid that things might be ending. I have been diagnosed with a very serious illness and I am treasuring every moment and I am terrified of what the world will be like, but even more so, I am terrified of what happens next.

I saw you over a video call and I hope you are holding on. You seem to be doing well, but I think you know more than you are letting on, having been in the hospital so many times yourself. You are only four years old, but you know full well what the paper bracelet on my arm means. You know about the tubes, the tests, the people in white coats and the sadness that their presence can mean.

When I was diagnosed, my first thought was that I regret absolutely nothing I did that may have put me at risk. There are many causes for cancer, some say up to one hundred combined factors. I am glad I did not live trying to hide from it. I do not regret all the times I travelled to Cambodia because I fell in love

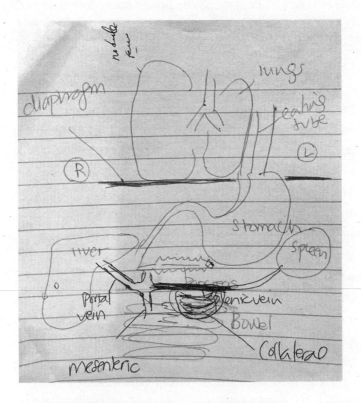

Diagram of my organs. Drawn by thrombosis doctor at
St. Paul's Hospital in Vancouver, November 4, 2021.

with the place. I do not regret the six years I lived in Hong Kong because that is where I met your father. I do not regret having a baby and risking myself with all the X-rays, because I gave birth to you. It was all worth it, and if anything I did caused this then I do not care. It doesn't matter. What matters is that I have you and your father and all the people around us who love us so, and that is what it means to live.

If I am not around to teach you, then your father and grand-parents will one day tell you that mama was born in a refugee camp where there was no clean milk and only contaminated food and water. In a way, mama lived forty-one years longer than she was supposed to. In a way, she beat the prognosis of war. So if you see mama in pain, don't be sad.

One night, you asked me, *Is mama in pain? Is it because of Kai?* This broke my heart a million times over. No, Kai, mama has never been in pain because of Kai: Kai has only brought her love and joy. Remember that war lives on within our bodies as well as our memories, and we are survivors of war. We are living on stolen time, and every moment we survive is a moment we are beating the odds.

In my hospital room I have a roommate named Ellen, a fairy godmother with large glasses whose husband died of cancer years after she herself was diagnosed with it. She tells me not to resist it, that the more you resist, the more it persists. Keep creating, she tells me. Build a new future. I think of you and believe we can still create a future together.

By the time you are old enough to read this, mama may not be here anymore. But I hope I can live to write another letter like this.

I hope that letter is about how different and difficult life has become, and not a goodbye.

love always,
your mom,
Nov 6, 2021

[anti-travel]

I trace the beginning of my mental unravelling to the night I was robbed on the streets of Phnom Penh.

It's June 2015. My partner Chris and I just finished dining on the Riverside. Earlier in the evening, Chris gave a reading at Java Cafe near the Independence Monument. He read from his novel-in-progress about Asian American expatriates travelling through Asia, their desires to make new lives for themselves in the countries their parents had left behind. When we first met in Hong Kong in 2014, I told him I loved the concept. What a brilliant idea to imagine the stories behind these new lines of flight. I asked him if Cambodia was a part of the story. He said, *of course it is*. Cambodia held a special place in his heart after his travels there in his early twenties.

As we leave the Riverside restaurant, Chris wants to hail a tuk-tuk to take us back to our hotel, but I insist that we walk. It's a beautiful night, I say. *Let's just walk. I've walked these streets a million times.* We turn down a side street near the National Museum and my alarm bells start to go off. I notice piles of garbage and few street lights. A young boy, no older than eight, runs up to us. I lock eyes with him and notice something in them, a watchfulness. Later, I will wonder, How did he know I wasn't Cambodian? Was it my clothes? Was it walking with Chris, who is half-white, and clearly isn't Cambodian? Would it have mattered anyway?

Before I know it, I hear the roar of a motorbike approach us from behind. I hear a snap and feel my purse being pulled off my arm. Two masked people on a motorbike have cut my purse strap with a bolt cutter. I scream and chase after them. We can't catch them on foot, so we jump into a tuk-tuk and I tell the driver to *GO!* The tuk-tuk starts but can't keep up with the speed of the motorbike. We lose them and the tuk-tuk driver says sorry, sheepishly. He lets us out and drives off quickly without asking for payment.

I feel shaken, disoriented, and angry. We get back to the hotel and I go online to erase my iPhone remotely. Around twenty minutes have elapsed since my purse sailed through the air. When we go downstairs to tell the hotel staff that we would like to report the theft to the police, they tell us that this would be futile. Some feeling inside me starts to stir again.

A Khmer girl in front of the Royal Palace, from the tourist pamphlet
A Shell Guide to Cambodia *by G. V. Smith, 1966. Photo by FARK.*

[shame]

Looking back now, I know that getting robbed in Phnom Penh wasn't really the beginning of my mental unravelling. But perhaps that's when the torch was lit, when the world inside me began to tilt and fray. Over the years, I would go back to the word "disintegrate." *I feel as though my brain is disintegrating.*

At the time, I didn't realize the unravelling, the terror I felt that night would get worse in the days to come as I became subject to identity theft, as the passwords on my accounts began to change one by one, as my linked devices—even the iPad that I had set up for my parents in Canada under my account—would get erased. I didn't realize how long it would take before I would feel comfortable walking at night in Phnom Penh, that I would wince every time I heard a motorbike drive up behind me.

I told this story about the robbery once to a colleague at a conference. *We need to be careful about the way we narrate thefts and robberies in Cambodia*, she told me. She believed I was lending credence to Western stereotypes by doing this. Shame enveloped me. How well academia had taught us to turn sad, personal moments into abstract theories. This minor incident, this little story, that meant nothing in comparison with what Cambodians endure on a daily basis, had nowhere to go but deeper within.

What does it mean to believe that something came undone in me that night? That more than just my strap was cut loose? That a violation had taken place? Can I, a privileged returnee with a Canadian passport, really mourn the loss of my sense of safety in a city that isn't mine to begin with? Yet this is how I feel.

For a long time, I felt that I had lost a place that I loved, or at least, I was grieving the convenient fiction that a place was all I needed to be free. No number of academic books telling me about the source of poverty and desperation could help me bring it back. It took many ventures back to Cambodia with friends, companions, and family, to renew my love for the place, and for myself.

*Advertisement of the 1906 Colonial Exposition in Marseilles, France,
depicting Khmer Apsara dancers alongside other icons of other colonial
pavilions staged at the exposition (via Wikimedia Commons).*

[refuge]

The more I look back at the night of the robbery, the more I wonder if I was cursed that day. That morning, I had entered Wat Langka to conduct research for my book. I forgot to take my shoes off, and I was on my period. I had taken photos of urns full of ashes of people who had died during Pol Pot time. Not being a particularly superstitious person, I had committed sacrilege on many levels. When I told these things to my mother, she immediately told me to go to a temple. I should burn some incense and say some prayers to cast off what I had brought on.

Before the robbery, I had been feeling better than I had for most of my life. It was my third year living in Hong Kong, a restless city that had brought me anonymity and freedom. In Hong Kong's steamy, meandering streets, the responsibilities and burdens of the past felt far away at last. I was an ocean away from my mother's screams. I felt I had finally found that distance I sought from Canada, and the proximity I wanted to Cambodia.

Phnom Penh was an intoxicating refuge, a city that I had begun to visit obsessively, making the short flight from Hong Kong an almost weekly ritual. I told myself that the city would give me what

I had always longed for: I would learn the Khmer language and one day converse fluently with my parents; I would connect with the Cambodian side of my family and be part of a community I never had; I would make the city a part of me wholly and completely, taking in every dish, every song, every film, every new friend.

I took Chris along with me in my passion to absorb the city. Together, we zipped across Phnom Penh with our tuk-tuk driver Tuol, frequenting our favourite spots: Boeung Kak, the Bophana Center, the Riverside, BKK1, Meta House, the Central Market, Tuol Tompoung, the Empire theatre. At night we danced at Blue Chilli, Heart of Darkness, and Pontoon. We took weekend trips to the seaside towns in the south, wandering through the ruins of Bokor Mountain, the sleepy streets of Kep and Kampot, and the quiet beaches of Sihanoukville.

Later, when my friends Maddie and Thy visited Cambodia with us, we would take pride in taking them to all our spots. Cambodia awakened all our senses, fuelled our passions and bodies. The scenes we saw in this new Cambodia being "reborn" or "coming out of the shadows" broke our hearts every day, but for the first time in my life, I actually felt lucky for everything I had.

I follow my mother's advice. I go to the temple. I burn incense and say some prayers. But I do not ask the gods to cast off anything. I still love this city and I still long to be part of it. Instead, I ask for forgiveness.

[eat]

2014. At the Patio Hotel in Phnom Penh, Chris comes into our room from the pool while I'm writing. *North Koreans*, he says. *There are North Koreans basking by the pool. Just chatting away on their iPhones.* Somehow this image seems funny and, given the "Axis of Evil" talk we grew up with, out of place.

Our research on Google for "North Koreans in Phnom Penh" brings us to another out-of-place place, the Pyongyang Restaurant in Phnom Penh, one of many chain restaurants led by the North Korean government. Inside, we watch North Korean women in traditional hanboks serve food and perform music and folk dances, largely for a clientele of Chinese and South Korean tourists. As we chew from side dishes of kimchi and radish, I begin to wonder about how spaces like this bear the traces of Cambodian, Chinese, and North Korean fraternities—that is, the flows of ideas, arms, and people. I wonder about my own tourist ethics of patronizing the restaurant, with its projection of women virtuosos and its flow of capital back to Pyongyang.

[panorama]

In 2018, I visit the Angkor Panorama Museum in Siem Reap, a US$24 million project funded by the North Korean government's Mansudae Overseas Projects Group. A monument to the little-known Cold War friendship between Cambodia and North Korea, it is the largest and most expensive museum in Cambodia. Its centrepiece is a 120-metre mosaic painted by North Korean artists in celebration of the ancient Khmer empire.

Walking through small crowds of Chinese tourists, I think about the comfortable portrait of Cambodia's past conjured up here for visitors, about the missing images of fraternity, and about the uneven landscape of memorialization in Cambodia's present in which so many wartime tragedies still cannot be grieved.

How do we remember the Cold War from a place like Cambodia, a place that still must shape and reshape its own history not just for Western tourists, but also for various Asian audiences?

I think of the Tumen River, which separates North Korea and China, a place that witnesses many refugees fleeing from the East, while from the West comes the deportation of many of these defectors.

Angkor Panorama Museum, Siem Reap, Cambodia, August 2018.
Photo by Y-Dang Troeung.

I think of the transformation of Cambodia's once-sleepy beach town, Sihanoukville, at one time turned into a focal point of China's One Belt One Road policy, and now an abandoned metropolis full of half-built casinos and hotels.

I think of the forced deportation of Uyghur asylum seekers from Cambodia to China, of North Korean ships of Scud missiles flying under Cambodia's flag of convenience and destined for Yemen.

I think too of the casual, unseeing passage of tourists through restaurants and museums. I wonder why some seem so bizarre, so out of place, while others do not.

[red]

My father often describes his days as a student in Cambodia in the early 1960s as the years when *Cambodia started becoming red*. Attending an ethnic Chinese high school in Kampong Thom, my father's school curriculum changed after Mao Zedong came to power in China. Cambodian students began every morning reading the Little Red Book and reciting slogans in Chinese such as "Americans are Paper Tigers." They learned about how China had heroically sent a Volunteer Red Army to fight against the Americans during the Korean War. When Chinese Communist Party leaders such as Zhou Enlai or Liu Shaoqi travelled to Phnom Penh, all the students in my father's school bused to the capital city to line the streets and join in the ceremonial welcome.

The vivid image of Chinese state visits to Cambodia in my father's memories mirrors the scenes that can be found in the archives of Prince Norodom Sihanouk's visit to North Korea in 1971, one year after the Cambodian head of state was ousted by a US-backed coup. In exile in the streets of Pyongyang, Sihanouk waved from his escorted convertible to crowds of North Korean greeters holding red and white balloons. Sihanouk sought

1974, the road to Oudong. The heart-shaped dance floor of a once-fashionable country club had become a repository for an international display of captured weapons—Chinese rocket launchers, Russian AK-47s, and American M16s. Photo by Colin Grafton. Courtesy of the photographer.

refuge in a mansion built for him by Kim Il Sung, calling him his "true brother."

Later, Sihanouk described his transits back and forth between his homes in Pyongyang and Beijing through the language of Asian brotherhood: *You have to know that I am an Asian man—I am a yellow man, not a white man. So I am guided by sentimental feelings, by feelings of gratitude, and it is those that are most important to me. I will always be grateful to my hosts here, and in China, for giving me everything when everything was lost.* A refugee himself, Sihanouk placed all his trust in his new hosts, and rallied the Cambodian people to support the Khmer Rouge. This effort to please his hosts, his new brothers, proved to be disastrous for all Cambodian people, including Sihanouk himself.

Even as Chinese engineers began to flow into Cambodia from 1975 to 1979, sent over to consult on the agricultural projects of Pol Pot's "Super Great Leap Forward," the Khmer Rouge were disappearing ethnic Chinese themselves, as well as any Cambodians caught speaking a Chinese language. My father witnessed this betrayal, as the ethnic Chinese in Cambodia, mostly Teochew people, who had once committed themselves to Mao's revolution, were not spared the cruelty of the Khmer Rouge. Speaking Chinese—a sign of Communist revolt in some parts of the world—in Cambodia, was construed as a sign of education, and marked one against the Communist revolution.

[tours]

In my many visits to the Tuol Sleng Genocide Museum over the years, I have noticed more groups of Chinese tourists. I wonder what it is like for those living within the People's Republic to come face to face with the shattered remains of a laboratory of Communist ideology, one that took direct inspiration from Mao Zedong's Great Leap Forward with Pol Pot's Super Great Leap Forward, a massive experiment that worked people to the point of exhaustion, illness, and death.

For my family, China and Cambodia were never distinct, nor could they be separated from our colonial past. Our surname comes from the Chinese surname Zhang (张), transliterated by French colonialists in the 1930s from the Teochew surname Teo (张) to Troeung. In Canada, my parents give me a Chinese first name and characters, Yilan (依蘭), referring to ylang-ylang, the perfumed yellow flowers that derive from *Cananga odorata*, a tropical tree with roots in India, Cambodia, Laos, Vietnam, the Philippines, Malaysia, and Indonesia. In Chinese, my full name is Zhang Yilan, 張依蘭.

China and Cambodia have a deeply embedded history. But here at Tuol Sleng, this place of unimaginable torture, history is transformed into a hall of mirrors, separating nations into morbid reflections. The tourists hope to capture pictures of a horror that cannot be fathomed. Cambodian tour guides at Tuol Sleng adjust their scripts to bury accounts of past complicities. They say, *Cambodia and China are friends now. Do not talk about the past.*

[utopia]

King Sihanouk was not the only outsider seeking a new Communist fraternity. In Pol Pot time, Cambodia remained closed to the rest of the world with the exception of leftist tour groups such as the Sweden-Kampuchea Friendship Association, who had been sympathetic toward the Chinese revolution and Mao Zedong. Like those who marched in the streets of Paris waving Mao's Little Red Book in 1968, these traveller-comrades were enticed by the lure and romance of a Communist utopia. They arrived in Democratic Kampuchea believing they had found a true egalitarian state.

In Pol Pot's Cambodia, Western tour groups encountered a staged reality, projections that met their illusions of a Communist utopia. Their tourist photos became a part of Pol Pot's propaganda, disseminated for all the world to see that all was right and just in Kampuchea. In hindsight decades later, after millions of Cambodian deaths and irrefutable evidence of atrocities, many of those who once refused to see beyond the façade expressed regret at their love affair with a red Cambodia. *For my part in this I am deeply sorry*, wrote one Western repentant, Gunnar Bergstrom, a photojournalist who visited in 1978 and whose photos were used to help deny accusations of human rights abuses and atrocities. *But I can't turn back history.*

[circuit]

It is May 2018. Again, I am at Tuol Sleng Genocide Museum. With each visit I've made to this space in the past decade, I've noticed a change in the atmosphere. With each visit, I find myself able to walk a little longer. I feel less disoriented, more contemplative. There is more information available, or maybe I am able to see it for the first time.

At the entrance, I am given an audio device for the museum. I hear a Khmer voice:

You've just entered a place of nightmares, filled with dreadful things that happened from 1975–1979. I'm here to tell you about them. My name is Ros Kosal. I am Cambodian. I will never forget those terrible years. From my family of nine only four survived. My two brothers and three of my sisters have never been found.

I am drawn in by Ros's voice. I feel that for the first time I am being differently grounded, anchored in a space that has always thrown me off balance. Ros's voice warns me that what I'm about to see inside the museum is *extremely distressing* and that I *may want to listen to the audio guide outside the site*. His gentle voice explains that this museum is a *documentation for all humankind*, and that after I leave this space, I *too will be a keeper of memory*.

Courtyard of Tuol Sleng Genocide Museum. To Those Who Are No Longer Here *(2017), statue by Séra. Photo by Y-Dang Troeung.*

I notice many people sitting on benches in the courtyard, silently listening to Ros's voice on their audio guides. They sit facing the centre of the courtyard, looking at a bronze sculpture of a figure frozen in mid-air, tumbling backwards with its hands pressed together in the gesture of a sampeah. It is a memorial to the victims of the Khmer Rouge, created by French Cambodian artist Séra Ing. I recall that Séra's father disappeared during the fall of Phnom Penh after being denied access into the French embassy to follow his French wife and mixed-race son who had taken refuge there.

Again, I think about my uncle, who boarded a plane in 1975 to help build a new Cambodia. I think about his children in Russia with whom I have never been able to make contact.

I walk through Building B and stop at Exhibit 9, "The Arrival of Kampuchea Democratic, 1975." I see images of Phnom Penh in the years before the fall. Ros's voice explains that *there were as many as three million people living here. More than half were refugees from battles between Khmer Rouge and Lon Nol forces, and also from the eight years of American bombing of Cambodia. It was part of their war with Vietnam. In the US, bombing Cambodia was called the secret war. It was no secret here.*

I think about my father, mother, and brothers taking refuge in a pagoda during the secret war. I remember my father's escape from Kampong Thom to Phnom Penh by boat in 1973. I see all the secrets, aliases, and reinventions that enabled them to survive in the following years.

I stop at the panel of foreigners killed at S-21. On the audio guide, I go to the tribunal recording of the Civil Party testimony of Rob Hamill, the brother of Kerry Hamill, a New Zealander whose boat was attacked by a Khmer Rouge gunboat off the coast of Cambodia in 1978. Hamill was captured, transferred to Tuol Sleng, tortured, and killed. His story is told in the film *Brother Number One*.

I walk by the image of Hout Bophana. She is known as the Anne Frank of Cambodia, but I wonder how accurate this comparison is. Anne Frank is known the world over; Hout Bophana has barely registered in the archive of twentieth-century genocides.

I come to the section of the museum devoted to Vann Nath, stopping at the self-portrait that I first saw in 2008 on the cover of the record book given to me and my mother at Tuol Sleng. I listen to Ros tell me that *perhaps our courageous and gentle artist Vann Nath should have the final word here.* The audio guide ends with Ros's recounting of Vann Nath's words referring to Angkar, the Communist Party of Kampuchea: *If everyone only thinks of Angkar—Discipline. Order. Carry out orders or be killed—it's the end of the world. It's the end of justice. There are no more ideals. No more human conscience.*

I exit the interior of the compound and enter the courtyard, where two children are playing in the bright-green grass. I picture bringing my son, just eight months old, here one day to learn about his grandparents' history of survival. I walk up to a memorial piece where the names of the dead have been engraved into grey stone slabs. I notice the overgrown, brilliant-green mango trees that create a canopy from the sun. I look up at the large palm trees swaying against the blue sky. I am surprised that I now find the space peaceful, beautiful.

[rodeo]

When I tell my therapist about my cancer diagnosis, he says that I have been equipped to face death. *This is clearly not your first rodeo*. I ask him what he means.

My therapist has seen a lot of people in tragic moments. He says my family seems to be well-practised at this. We take a tally of my life, and I'm amazed at having my own life, my own narration of my life, told back to me, in ways that mark its most tragic moments. Living through them, I never thought my life was a tragedy. For me and my partner, together, our lives have been magical and romantic, even in times of terror and misfortune. My therapist reassures me that my life is not tragic. But something about the tally he takes sticks with me. I realize that even though my daily life has been beautiful and joyous, from an outsider's point of view, it seems unfathomable, almost nauseating in its repetitious downward spiral.

My therapist's tallying gives me a version of my life as a set of strategies that were each developed to respond to a different crisis. Perhaps, he suggests, this is why I have chosen a career that demands I research the lives of the lost. This has been somewhat obvious to me as well—the way I engross myself in the lives of others because I don't want to see my own as a series of tragedies. This research makes me feel, distanced as I am, that I can share my own suffering with them, that we understand our pain together. We share the burden.

But being alone inside the gravity of others has weighed me down. Now, I must take on my own tragedy, and on its own terms. Living one day at a time is maddening. It's the slow drip of torture, the wearing down of the daily checkpoints, the chipping away of your self-defences, the degree-by-degree boiling of the frog's pool, the welling up of anger. The spiral I'm in has meant that every bit of bad news I receive pushes me closer to an edge that I'm too afraid to look at directly. I know if I did, the depths below would come into focus.

He tells me that sometimes I may feel like I'm in a burning house and running toward the fire. But around me people will continue to live their lives, busying and worrying, while I will regret not being able to participate in all the pivotal things that life can offer. The machinations of the world will go on, and I will seem so far from them; just acknowledge it and accept that it's happening.

We return, as usual, to my book. The void that swallows and swallows. I tell him how I always joke, *I'll be dead before my first book ever comes out!* Now, it turns out I'm probably right. He asks how I feel about this. I tell him, in a way, it's actually a dream come true. I can write and publish a book, and never have to do a talk or an interview about it. My work can mean what it means, do what it does, and for the first time ever, I can steer clear of the spotlight.

[student]

I am thirty-two when I arrive in Hong Kong in 2012, having accepted a job here without ever visiting the place. I've just surprised my peers by cutting short a fully funded post-doctoral fellowship at the University of Southern California, where I worked with Viet Thanh Nguyen, one of the wisest and most capable scholars in my field. Despite my own doubts, both Viet and my supervisor understand my final decision. Hong Kong will be an experience far beyond studying in Southern California.

Before I left North America, a colleague told me, *I can't believe we work in a profession that forces you to move so far away, to another continent!* Her words stick with me. What some see as a failure, I see as opportunity, freedom, the chance for new discoveries and connections. Here, in Hong Kong, I can learn everything over; here I can unlearn; here I can be close to Cambodia.

I soon realize upon arriving that I am a member of a growing roster of Western professors working in Asia. But unlike most of them, I embody an uncanny image for the students in my classroom. I physically pass as a local Hong Kong citizen, yet I have a different set of roots and routes than my students, the majority of whom have lived their whole lives in Hong Kong. It is not uncommon for students to ask me with sincere curiosity why I do not speak Chinese or if I was brought up learning Chinese cultural traditions.

I try to turn my students' questions into teaching moments and prod them to reflect on the texts in the course and the themes of immigration, assimilation, and refugee experience. Eventually, my students acquire an understanding of the harm that words such as *authenticity* and *purity* have had on how we see ourselves and others.

When my students discover I am a refugee, I become part of their wider family. Many of them, I discover, are the children of refugees from China, many of whom swam or took boats across the Deep Bay. Some came from war, some from famine, some from pollution, some because they or their parents had crossed some sacred sexual boundary. For the first time, when I tell my story of movement and desperation to a classroom, I am met with a dozen other similar stories.

The students in my first course, Asian Literatures in English, tell me they've never had a literature course like this: about Asia, about their own histories, taught by an Asian woman. I tell them I've never been able to teach a course like this, or to students who would embrace rather than distance themselves from it.

When the class ends, we all gather for a class photo. I've never done this before, but I feel elated by the hugs and smiles and hand signals and, afterwards, the giddy screams in Cantonese that punctuate the halls as students swipe over each image. With so much to learn and unlearn, I am a student once again.

Border of the Causeway Bay Occupy Central encampment, 2014.
Photo by Y-Dang Troeung.

[occupy]

Hong Kong is an active place, a city where activism is present in every word, every gesture.

I am elated to live here. The art of action is here, and it is all-embracing.

[home work]

I am part of the movement, watching police tear down the barricades that have protected this space. It's been nearly three months since Umbrella Movement protestors occupied Causeway Bay. The police are repeating the same announcement over a megaphone. A young man translates for me and explains that they are ordering people to evacuate the area or else face arrest. I'm a foreigner. If I am arrested, I will be deported.

I move my way to the front of the line and sit down with the crowd. Wordlessly, we acknowledge each other. Some are students. I watch them pull out their homework and read their books in silence. They are solving math puzzles and writing essays, and they remain defiant.

I am in awe of their courage, their youth, and the futures they are risking in this moment.

The police close in. I stand up to take a photo, hoping to bear witness to whatever might occur. A Hong Kong auntie standing behind the students yells at the police, shaming them for betraying the city's youth. Even as an outsider, I understand her anger, her need to protect these brave kids who all look like my students.

The last day of the Occupy Central encampment, 2014.
Photos by Y-Dang Troeung.

A white man, a British colonial police officer, stands silently, seemingly in charge. He gives an order and the police force themselves upon us. Everything around me swirls. All I hear is noise, but I am up and I am fleeing.

Somehow I make my way to the MTR, tears streaming down my face. The subway is packed, and I feel anonymous again. A young man who is squeezed up against me offers me a tissue. He tells me not to cry. The whole city is mourning today.

[corrections]

After the end of the Occupy Central movement, I begin to teach my students more about their local refugee histories rather than my own or those in North America. I find that these too are not so different.

Beginning in 1975, Hong Kong received more than 200,000 "boat people" fleeing the Vietnam War. While the Hong Kong government initially set up open camps allowing Vietnamese refugees the freedom to temporarily work outside the camps, by 1982, the government held these refugees in closed centres: converted factories, military sites, and prisons. The government subjected them to arbitrary, controversial screenings, and asked them to tell their stories again and again. If these stories were not to the satisfaction of the correctional officers, the refugees were cast out of *legitimate refugee* status to that of *economic migrant*. Once denied refugee status, refugees were repatriated en masse beginning in 1989. The last camp in Hong Kong, Pillar Point refugee camp, closed in 2000, over twenty-five years after the end of the Vietnam War.

My Hong Kong students encounter this history as simultaneously familiar and foreign. I cannot find a single student who knows of it in any detail; instead, they vaguely recall the way these refugees were cast as lazy and good-for-nothing. I tell them I have heard these words too. They cast the many outcasts who haunt the collective memory of a nation that rejects them.

We read Andrew Lam's journalistic essay of the Hong Kong camps, "The Stories They Carried," and watch scenes from Ann Hui's film *Boat People*. We discuss the abject conditions of the camps and the barrage of stories from refugees looking to communicate their plight to the world. We talk about how the Vietnamese refugees, like many of the students who also see themselves as refugees and immigrants, carry stories and traditions with them, and how the ideas of desperate, pitiable refugees ignore all this.

When the class ends, I am uncertain what this history might mean to them. As I write this, there are hundreds of thousands of refugees in Hong Kong from around the globe, many working in underground economies, as sex workers or dancers, or as domestic workers who are, by law, required to live with their employer. And so soon after the handover to the People's Republic of China and the still-traumatic—and beautiful—memories of the Occupy movement, who can blame my students for not knowing about closed camps that the media once discussed as public eyesores?

Still, I feel close to my students, even in their lack of knowledge about this history. I too am still learning it. Eagerly, we try and try to understand.

Journalists were, by and large, barred from entry to this place known for riots and gang fights and mass protests and a handful of self-immolations. There were eleven people, mostly women, who disemboweled themselves in protest of being forced back. The place, divided into sections, is built like a maximum security prison. Barbed wire on top of five-meter-high chicken wire fences.

—Andrew Lam, "The Stories They Carried"

[excursion]

It's 2018, and I'm in my final year in Hong Kong. This is the last time I will bring my students to Cambodia, to this month-long study-abroad excursion in Siem Reap.

Getting the students to Cambodia for the third year in a row has been eye-opening. My students, who would not see themselves as Asian but as Hong Kongers, still take on the global imaginary of Asia. They see Cambodia as a tragic country; a zone of inhumanity to be solved through humanitarian development; a place for a cheap holiday sojourn amidst exotic temples and dark tourism; or, finally, a new frontier for foreign investment and wild speculation.

I don't blame my students for this. On the trial runs before our excursion, we meet with an NGO worker who leads the English-teaching branch in Siem Reap. She recommends a book to the students, one that I know well. It is one of many victim-blaming books that attribute Cambodia's modern history of suffering to an affliction of cultural traits—namely, passivity and violence—inherent to the nation's people.

I take my students through the marketplaces, telling them the history of a time when Cambodia was called the "Pearl of Asia" and an "Island of Peace." I catch a glimpse of their phones. They are not looking up histories, but the best bars and clubs to hit after the market.

After I leave them at their homestay I wander about, and find some of them in hotel pools, laughing and kicking water. Three students are feeling intense stomach pains and fight each other for the bathroom. Others are distraught at having to do something they never expected to do on this trip: sweep floors and clean their own dishes.

I worry about how they will continue to perceive this place when we leave. As a curse, a tourist playland, or a place of histories and peoples similar to their own?

Anida Yoeu Ali, Enter the Ruins, Enter *series (Archival Inkjet Print, 2012).*
Photo by Vinh Dao. Courtesy of Studio Revolt.

[letter]

On our last day in Siem Reap, I let the NGO worker take the students to the Angkor Wat temples so I can walk the city and visit my favourite cafés and museums. I search for a temple, in need of something to bring closure to my time here. It's 2018, and I'm about to move to Vancouver, Canada, which will take me further from Cambodia than I have been in the past six years. Six years of constant, sometimes monthly, sometimes weekly, excursions. Six years of making friends and reuniting with family, of renting my own apartment in Phnom Penh and maintaining ties to artists, poets, organizers, performers, and other refugees.

I see text messages from my students, more about their stomach pains. Some complain about the humidity. I don't know how to tell them not to trust the NGO workers, who have sacrificed so much to try to do good in the world, but do so from a misinformed place. I want to tell them that Cambodians under Pol Pot time were not passive, but became versatile in the arts of flexibility, adaptability, and resourcefulness; in bending their minds and bodies beyond capacity to survive. I want to explain how my parents had to cross checkpoints and borders to find refuge, and how we had to navigate immigration, racism, and resettlement, and how we all still fight to keep our children and elders alive. I want to tell my students my mother's story about *kamleang chet*, her feeling that propelled acts of refusal: not to die and not to let her children die. I try to put the words together, but my tears rush faster than the first letter.

When night falls, my partner Chris spirits me to a drag bar. The stage lights up with music and vivid colours of gold and purple, and the performers are in their element, with hoots and claps from a nearly all-Cambodian audience. When a song comes on to end the night, I recognize it instantly. It's the music of Ros Serey Sothea, the 1960s pop star, the queen with the golden voice, who was later disappeared by the Khmer Rouge. Her song is a romantic ballad turned dance number, amped up for the people in this joyous crowd who stand, clapping.

The lights black out to a chorus of cheers. Ros Serey Sothea's voice remains, flowing up and down in small waves that bounce off the walls and through the microphones of the onstage performers. Sothea was once my parents' music, the songbird of their past. In this room, in this place, we feel her still, the disappeared we can never leave behind.

Dearest Kai,

This letter is for your fifth birthday, though it is still seven months away. I am writing to you now, in case I am not here to see it.

Your father read somewhere of a man who also had an incurable cancer, and wrote letters to his son in the future, so that even in death he could offer advice. I don't know what life will be like in your future, if this pandemic will have gone away by then, or if I will, miraculously, still be alive to celebrate this birthday with you. I have come to learn, within the past month of doctor's visits, surgeries and prognoses, that certainty does not grow straight and tall like rice stalks; it grows like wayward vines that must rely on something unknown to keep their grip, whether it be a thousand-year-old tree, or a concrete building slated for demolition.

Our certainty has been tossed to the grounds of a language that is consistent yet ever-shifting. The phrase *good outcome*, we have learned, is infinitely flexible. It once meant a clean X-ray. Then it meant a benign growth. Then it meant that the thing inside me could be removed. Then, a *good outcome* meant years. Now, it means months. What once meant survival, remission, is now a quicksand of uncertain futures.

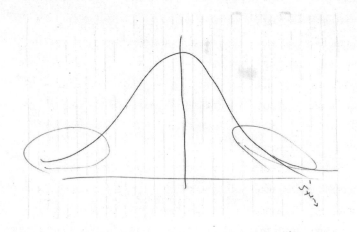

Hand-drawn prognosis by my pancreatic cancer oncologist.
BC Cancer–Vancouver, November 16, 2021.

I know in this past year of your life, your grandparents will help you deal with these uncertainties. They have overcome many, and they know that life will always continue to grow. Though your grandfather is often silent, his eyes speak in shiny orbs that hold a universe of memories, and you only need but ask to pluck them out. Your grandmother, when I told her of what was happening to me, said *it's unbelievable. It's just like a bomb that went off somewhere.* Your grandparents still see bombs, and they have learned well how to survive with the uncertainty that bombs can bring. Your grandparents know that the disease I fight now is linked, in unknowable ways, to the war they once fled. Their lives were upended by bombs and chemicals, mine by the toxins that bombs and chemicals create. These mechanisms, which were there in my beginning, will be there at my end.

Remember that your grandparents are storytellers, and for them, telling stories is not being stuck; it is healing and learning and understanding. Over the past weeks, they have told me many stories of the people they've known who had the same illness as me, almost without any forethought or order. They've told me about whether these people survived, lived long, or died within weeks. All the stories come.

Stories of the dead and suffering need not drop you in stillness. They can instead show us that our very lives are miracles, that every day since Pol Pot time has been a gift. Our family has always lived that way.

Your laughter remains the heartbeat of our little household, and I am beginning to understand how life would be so much emptier without you in it. In a funny way, pondering my own death has opened up new capillaries toward love. It is similar to having a child—the opening up of the soul, the new ways of loving and seeing each other. My only regret is not living to see what other ways love can so radically return in new, unexpected ways.

Your father and I love you more than anything. You keep us strong and united, and you make every day a joy. Thank you for being your special, lovable self.

love always,
your mom

[confer]

July 2019.

I am in Phnom Penh, at an international conference on geno-cide studies, a gathering of over five hundred scholars from around the world. For the first time in the organization's history, the conference is being held in Cambodia.

I'm on edge, incapable of calming my mind. I feel waves of nervousness being here on the other side of the world, away for the first time from my two-year-old son who has a rare medical condition. Over the past year, since his illnesses began, a new level of mental agitation has set in. I feel as though I have stopped sleeping almost entirely. One doctor believes I have untreated postpartum depression. Another tells me I have PTSD from witnessing my child's medical emergencies. I read obsessively about the epigenetic transmission of trauma, asking my son's doctors, all ten of them, about the possibility that his condition stems from the methylation caused by histories of violence.

My therapist doesn't offer any official diagnoses for me, but he tells me I can't hold all the things that have been accumulating, for years, perhaps decades, any longer. I agree with his assessments.

But I do nothing to slow things down. I'm at the beginning of a new job, a new start, just hanging on by a thread. So many are depending on me, so much remains unfinished. I can't afford to stop.

[program]

I ride a tuk-tuk for thirty minutes to the university where the conference is being held. Along the way, I observe the rapidly changing cityscape of Phnom Penh and think about the war raging on in Syria. I imagine what it would be like forty years from now, when Syria is a different place, if hundreds of Western scholars were to descend upon the country to present their expert interpretations of the atrocities happening now. All week I have been listening to authoritative speakers explain Cambodia's history to me and other Cambodians. Finally, at one conference panel, a young Cambodian student seemed fed up, and stood to voice his frustration at a panel of speakers: *I appreciate your analysis and look forward to reading your book, if it will be made available here. But I would like to ask you now, Where was your country when the genocide was happening?*

I recall the grumblings I heard in the lead-up to the conference about how difficult it was to make this historic event happen. *The Cambodians need to do something to organize their own conference*, one organizer said. *We can't do everything for them.*

I flip through the conference program and notice the dozens of presentations listed on the topic of Tuol Sleng. The academic obsession with this space—the scores of scholarly books, articles, and talks that it has generated—never ceases to amaze me. Articles written by scholars from the West, such as "The Authoritative Guide to the Tuol Sleng Museum of Genocidal Crimes," continue to get churned out year after year. It is not enough for them to write about Tuol Sleng. Reproducing the Tuol Sleng mug shots over and over again in their articles, some have turned the sheer amount of academic knowledge about Tuol Sleng into a topic of academic inquiry itself. Is it a morbid fascination with the macabre? An easy pretext for a holiday in Cambodia? A self-righteous quest to "give back"? An abstract fetishization of the dark aesthetic? Tuol Sleng seems to offer all of the above.

If tourists feel a sense of catharsis for having gone to the Killing Fields, how do scholars of Cambodia feel when writing their endless treatises on Tuol Sleng? But perhaps I am too cynical.

Anida Yoeu Ali, Roll Call, *from* The Buddhist Bug *series*
(Archival Inkjet Print, 2014). Photo by Vinh Dao. Courtesy of Studio Revolt.

[oun]

After the first full conference day, I visit my friend Anida, a Cambodian American artist and poet, on a rooftop patio. She tells me to look at the new and developing skyline full of glitzy new towers, made with investors from China, Japan, Singapore, and South Korea—*what seems Cambodian about this?* she asks me. I cannot say.

She tells me I look shaken, in disarray. I tell her *I'm not doing well, Bong.* I can't keep up with academia, my work, being a mother, caring for my aging parents, and also coming to conferences like this.

You need to slow down, oun. I feel the warmth of the word *oun*, little sister, younger cousin. *They say academia kills your maternal instinct.* She is a mother of three girls, who were raised partially in Phnom Penh. But by *maternal instinct*, I think she means more than our need to mother children. She means our need, when it comes to our histories, to reach beyond study and research. To care, to honour, to love. To mother, to sister, to cousin.

How can these Western scholars even begin to understand our history, or our work?

The industrial noise of an erecting skyscraper continues from a cluster of high-rises. Its discordant sounds blend with the chimes of a nearby wat. For now, I am calm.

———

[noise]

On the second day of the genocide conference, I find myself in a room listening to a panel of three speakers discussing aesthetics, the law, and Cambodia. The audience consists mostly of Western intellectuals—a mixture of academics, NGO workers, and lawyers involved in the Extraordinary Chambers in the Courts of Cambodia (ECCC) tribunal. The speakers themselves are trained as lawyers. A handful of Cambodians are present in the room. One of the presenters, a smartly dressed woman with brown hair and black-rimmed glasses, speaks about her recently published book on *who gets to decide who gets to be a victim*. As she speaks, a slideshow of images plays on rotation behind her.

A panel of three S-21 mug shots—photos of three young Cambodian girls captured and tortured at Tuol Sleng—fills up the entire projection screen, dwarfing the three presenters at the front of the room.

Every couple of minutes the S-21 images appear again, a dizzying rotation. The girls in the photos, depicted on the precipice of their death, remain unidentified. They are background wallpaper for this woman's presentation. One of the panellists shrinks in embarrassment. A mug shot in the middle of the panel shows a girl no older than twelve wearing a white uniform shirt and a number "3" tag. I wonder if her loved ones are still searching for her, where they are in the world, if they are present in the room today.

I feel the distortion of time and space around me. I hear people speaking, but I can't understand their words. The room is full of incomprehensible noise.

[verveine]

I make my way back to the conference to deliver my own presentation, a paper on "Emotional Survival during Pol Pot Time." When I'm up there, in front of that room full of experts with hostile eyes, I find I can barely speak, as if I'm being strangled from within. My mouth is completely dry. My hands and voice tremble embarrassingly. I am unable to look up at the audience, even for a moment. I muddle through the presentation, but my emotional breakdown is laid bare for all to see.

I am grateful for my friends Keiko and Colin, who skip the rest of the conference and ride the tuk-tuk back to Phnom Penh with me. I first met Colin many years earlier, when he approached me at a filmmaker's talk at Meta House, a German-Cambodian cultural centre, theatre, art gallery, café, and bar in Phnom Penh. The film was *Waiting for Cambodia*, a 1988 film about Site 2, which was the largest refugee camp on the Thai-Cambodian border, and for a time the largest in all of Southeast Asia. During the Q & A, I asked the film's director, David Feingold, if he had any footage from camp Khao-I-Dang, as I had yet to see any. He had none, but a man in front of me turned around and said, *I was there in 1980.*

*Khmer classical dance classes for teenagers in the temporary hospital at
Khao-I-Dang. Taken in 1980 by Colin Grafton, a volunteer relief worker
in Cambodian refugee camps alongside the Thai border. Since 2014,
Colin and his wife Keiko have worked on exhibitions and projects at the
Bophana Center, Tuol Sleng Genocide Museum, and Meta House.
Courtesy of the photographer.*

I have plenty of photos. I learned his name was Colin, and he had been in camp Khao-I-Dang as a relief worker with the World Food Programme. The photos were sitting in a file he had kept all these years, just waiting to be exhibited someday. *Would you like to see them?*

Today, Colin notices that I am a different person, my optimism and confidence sheared away. We sit down for a Japanese lunch and I ask if they can help me somehow. *Please help me.* I don't even know what I need help with, but it's all tangled together. I tell them I feel like I haven't slept for months; my life is a mess, even though everyone probably thinks it's perfect.

You could try verveine tea, Colin says, with his trademark British humour. *But it looks like you need something much stronger, like valium!*

[trial]

August 7, 2014.

I am sitting in a courtroom near Phnom Penh. I am about to witness history in the making. The media around me are asking, Is this history for the world, or just for Cambodians?

In 2010, the ECCC convicted the first Khmer Rouge leader, Kaing Guek Eav, also known as Duch, of crimes against humanity. This landmark case has now been followed by the case against Nuon Chea, second-in-command to Pol Pot, and Khieu Samphan, who was Cambodia's head of state during the Khmer Rouge. The *New York Times* has described the case as the "largest and most complicated prosecution since Nuremberg in 1945."

Today is the day of the verdict. Tears stream down my face as the historical account is read out loud.

guilty for crimes against humanity and genocide

Despite my mixed feelings about the tribunal, I cannot deny that I too feel a palpable weight in the air about what this day represents for us, the survivors. The significance of this day for Cambodian people gathered inside and outside the auditorium is undeniable. This verdict means something affective and intangible. It means something for my mother, who is following the news from her home in Canada, to see if her brother's S-21 executioner will finally be held accountable for his crimes.

Since the inception of the ECCC in 2003, scholars (myself included) have questioned the value of the tribunal within the broader context of war and justice worldwide. Are the trials even necessary? Do these international courts—costing over US$300 million total—have any benefit to the Cambodian people, or are they merely a test of Western human rights laws? Are there more culturally specific forms of justice that are rooted in Cambodian tradition and daily practice? Can lifelong imprisonment come close to distributing justice for the millions of dead? And what of the difficult, existential questions about what had happened? Are we to forget that the entire moral and spiritual world of Cambodia was, from the US bombing onwards, turned upside down?

My partner Chris holds my hand as I continue to cry and more questions pour into my mind. What about the justice demanded from the Americans who bombed Cambodia, who turned everyday farmers into Khmer Rouge soldiers fighting for their right to live? Or what of the justice demanded from the North, the Communist cadres who oversaw, influenced, encouraged, and armed the Khmer Rouge, happy to let Cambodian people fight their hot wars for them?

I cannot cry enough tears for the closure that this trial does not bring. But what it does bring, the acknowledgement of our history, the evidence of our collective memories, I continue to carry.

[open]

Is existence, persistence, continuation, the opposite of closure?

I ask myself this question as I watch a panel of lawyers debate the ECCC's decision at Meta House. The lawyers discuss the legal designation of the term *genocide*. How can we call this a genocide, when genocide is defined as one racial or religious group against another? Is Communism a different race?

The Dutch lawyer for Nuon Chea rebukes the charges of crimes against humanity. *What about the United States, who bombed Cambodia? The US is contributing millions of dollars to the tribunal in order to cover up its own unredressed injuries.*

I'm beginning to lose hope in definitions, and perhaps in language itself. As the lawyers declare the importance of reserving certain words for some peoples and not others, I do not laugh or cry or shout. Instead, I marvel at what is happening before us in this country, at the machinations of an entire legal-humanitarian-academic industry, speaking for the millions of Cambodian people still left grieving with open wounds.

How do we respond? I am as silent as the survivors around me.

Mr. Kissinger/General Haig (tape)   (General Haig extremely difficult to hear)
December 9, 1970 8:50 p.m.
jlj

H: Yes sir.

K: I just had a call from our friend. First, he wants to know by noon tomorrow whether the Coast Guard is going to be court marshalled because if they are going to be court marshalled he can avoid all questions.

H: No they're not.

K: Why not?

H: I understand that they have decided that there was no criminal culpability involved.

K: Well, what are they going to do - reprimand them?

H: Yes. XXXXXXXXXXXXXXXXXX They'll use administrative _____
    you

K: Well XX better get a written report from Volpe by 10 o'clock tomorrow morning. Can you get that?

H: (Can't hear)

K: Two, he wants a massive bombing campaign in Cambodia. He doesn't want to hear anything. It's an order, it's to be done. Anything that flys on anything that moves. You got that?

H: (Couldn't hear but sounded like Haig laughing.)
                                    to find out, he wants
K: Thirdly, now hold on to your hat. He wants/an inventory of every prop plane that's suitable for operations out there. He wants a report on it by Saturday morning, for possible movement out there.

H: XXXXXXXXX For close air support.

K: Yes. That's actually not a bad idea. Fourthly, he's now gung ho on the operation. Have you got Moorer yet?

H: Yes, I talked with him.

K: Is he happier?

H: Much. I didn't go too far.

K: No, but did you tell him I talked to the President?

H: Yes, I did. I told him _____ *(completely unintelligible)*

DECLASSIFIED
Author. NND EO 12958
By: ___ NARA Date 6/11/04

Transcript from "the Kissinger Telcons," December 9, 1970, in which Kissinger instructs General Alexander Haig to carry out four instructions—including the B-52 bombing of Cambodia on the order of Richard Nixon (via The National Security Archive).

[exhibit]

June 2021. I am in Vancouver using all the virtual tools that have emerged during the COVID-19 lockdowns to organize an art exhibition that will take place at the Bophana Center in Phnom Penh. The exhibition is a collaboration among artists and writers in Vancouver, Phnom Penh, Paris, London, and Lowell, Massachusetts. To ease the stress of this endeavour, I have relied on the Bophana Center's director, Sopheap Chea, as well as my friends Colin and Keiko, who have been by my virtual side throughout 2020 and 2021.

The exhibition begins in one month, and I feel my mind begin to twist. But something keeps it from unravelling, as it has before. I envisioned this exhibition as a salve, a means of repair and healing. It will bring together the voices of artists, activists, and community members for a collective conversation focused on Cambodia's artistic renaissance. I put all my hopes into this event, as well as all my anger. I think of the ECCC trials, the tribunals, the history books, the conference presentations, the endless, endless programs. I seek to somehow push back against all of these through the events I'm organizing: a three-month photography exhibition, a screening of Rithy Panh's film *Site 2* (about the refugee camp of the same name), as well as a recorded interview with Panh, gallery talks, embassy visits, countless conversations (as well as disagreements), and a concluding virtual roundtable that will gather voices from across the Cambodian diaspora.

I speak to one of these voices, Davi Hyder, through a computer screen. I don't know Davi well, just that she is a survivor of the war, and now lives on a farm near Phnom Penh where she grows fifteen different types of mangoes! Over a spotty internet connection, Davi exudes a vibrant energy and enthusiasm, even as she shares her experience of building a bomb shelter under her house during the Cambodian Civil War, of the apocalyptic storm of violence that engulfed Cambodia when the Khmer Rouge took over, and of how she managed to escape from Cambodia but lived in anguish not knowing the fate of the family members she had left behind. She tells me too about her travels to the Cambodian refugee camps in Thailand when the border opened in 1979—how she quickly learned the Thai language, enlisted as a relief worker, and did what she could as one of the few Cambodian women workers in the camp who could help translate between Thai and Khmer. She wanted me to know that refugee women and girls had suffered the most in the camps. What she witnessed in the camps—the pain Cambodian women and girls endured, as well as the care and love they showed each other—had shaped her entire life's path from that point onwards.

I feel humbled by the intensity and compassion with which Davi speaks about her memories of the camps. I feel, perhaps for the first time, an optimism for something I am helping to create. Through this exhibition, stories like Davi's will circulate and tell difficult truths about how the violence of war continues even in camps meant to give relief and refuge. The exhibition's amateur photographs of families, performances, and dancers in the camps will counter the scenes of war and poverty snapped by well-known photojournalists. The roundtable discussions we publish will find readers worldwide who can join us in celebrating the rebirth, revival, and regeneration of Cambodian arts and culture in the afterlife of war.

Months later, before our virtual roundtable, Davi informs us that she has to withdraw due to illness. We later discover that she passed away after suffering from complications due to COVID-19. I am stunned and saddened, but Colin, who knew her since they both lived in Phnom Penh in the early 1970s, is devastated. Like Davi, so many in Cambodia suffer from the fourth wave of the Delta variant. The situation in Cambodia has been characterized by the lack of safe vaccine availability, especially in the rural countryside, where people like Davi lived; an inequitable medical care system; prolonged lockdowns; quarantine zones; heightened surveillance; security checkpoints; empty city streets; military patrols; and the sound of police megaphones blaring curfew orders throughout the streets.

The pandemic lays bare the reality that healing can never come all at once. The thin layer of scab holding back the past's unhealed wounds easily comes undone.

Dearest Kai,

If I am still here to see your tenth birthday, it means I am part of the eight percent of people who survive this cancer for over five years.

Being in chemotherapy, in a funny way, makes me relive many of the days I was pregnant with you. The nausea of treatment forces me to retreat back to the foods I remember eating only during pregnancy: cereals and oats and watermelon. Sometimes, when I realize the chemotherapy, the catheters, and the pills are the only things keeping me alive, I feel like I am in the same bubble incubator that was your first bed in this world, where you lay for five days until your life signs were stabilized. I find myself obsessing over the CT scans of my own tumours in the way I used to obsess over the ultrasounds of your frail body. "Intra-uterine growth restriction" was the diagnosis they gave me for why you were measuring so small in my womb. Back then, I would study your measurements over and over, wishing them bigger, eating anything I could to help you grow, gaining sixty pounds in hopes that the weight would be transferred to you. In the end, it made no difference to your birthweight—a mere five pounds. Now, my

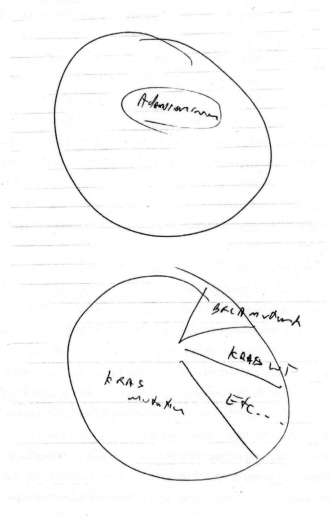

Hand-drawn diagram by my pancreatic oncologist at BC Cancer–Vancouver, November 16, 2021. Words: "Adenocarcinoma," "KRAS Mutation," "BRCA Mutant," "KRAS WT," "Etc. . ." This was written to explain new advances in Personalized Onco-Genomics that I might benefit from.

body is injected with toxic drugs that cause me to feel nauseous, weak, and fatigued, all to stop the growths, to cease the wayward life growing inside me.

In a strange way, your birth prepared me well for this illness, and I feel I can be strong against it. Mama may be in pain, and your memories of me may be of my discomfort, but know that I am happy to be alive and I want so desperately to live and be with you. The doctor helping me has become a kind spirit awaiting my recovery. He has dark, concave eyes, as if he is regularly punched after every prognosis he gives! Or does he just never sleep? Your father and I agree that his body language and appearance are very similar to your departed Uncle Don, and we feel comfortable in his presence. Like Don, the doctor is helping mommy through another difficult period.

Right now, in your life, chances are that your father is undertaking the monumental task of raising you. When I first met him, he was a twenty-eight-year-old boy, wearing black running shoes with green laces to a conference in Hong Kong. He has changed many times throughout his life, and I have always loved him for his flexibility. He moved to Hong Kong, he treated my parents like his own, and he agreed to move his whole life to Vancouver, only to deal with more challenges in our family's health. He has become a different person so many times. And he's doing it again right now, transforming before our eyes with the magic that our love can generate. I see him making new meanings out of this disease. Our love began with intensity and has been shot through with intensity ever since.

At ten years old, you are at an age where you will undergo life's biggest transformations. You have this ability in your family to change, to let your past self go so that your present self does not vanish into the background of a new place and time. We are a family gifted at the art of movement, of straying and sliding and striving. In a way, my illness too is an instance of being renamed, or of becoming unnamed.

Today my hair has begun to wiggle from my head and make little squiggles on the floor, as if you had taken a pen to doodle on the wood. I hope you do not sadden when you remember mama without hair—hair was always such a nuisance anyway! I hope you do not sadden when you remember me lying in bed all day or getting up only once to move through the motions and lumber about the house. I am always coming out of my little incubator to see you, and you bring me nothing but love, which is all I need to survive.

Love always,
your mom

[branch]

It's 2021, and my brother Meng still uses his Blackberry phone from 2010. So when he visits Vancouver with his daughter, my niece, Sophia, and my other brother, Pheng, he can't properly send or receive the photos we take together as a family. The family is stunned at my cancer diagnosis, but they still manage to keep things light and humorous for my sake.

Nearby our undecorated Christmas tree, we have a family discussion to plan what Meng's new phone should be, convincing him to finally catch up with the times. Where would we be without our apps? In one of our refugee non sequitur moments, our conversation turns from his phone to sports betting to Pol Pot time.

We didn't have Uber then, so why would I need it now?

When my brothers speak of Pol Pot time, they rarely share stories of hardship and terror. They might preface these stories with a description of the endless work hours and constant fear of losing their parents, as if to verify that this period was indeed terrible, that they did indeed spend their youth digging holes and cutting tree branches and carrying rocks, but they always brush these facts aside to clear a path for a much sillier and endearing memory.

Yeah it was terrible. We worked endlessly for all the hours of the day. But you know what was really funny about it . . .

Meng tells the story of when our brother, Pheng, was sitting on a tree branch collecting sticks. Nearing eleven, Pheng had been living for some months in a refugee camp, and because of the hardships of the Khmer Rouge work camps he *still wasn't all there.*

So he was up on this tree branch, high high up where no one could reach, and he's cutting away at all the branches around him with this small knife. Then he starts cutting away at the branch next to him—the branch he's sitting on! We're all watching him and laughing and telling him to stop but he keeps cutting until the branch comes out from under him and he falls right on his ass!

We're laughing at my brother while he laughs along, and we all laugh about the things that happened as they survived a mass genocide. Even as we laugh, I still wonder how many of the scars my brothers received during Pol Pot time were from a branch.

[rambo]

Raised in Pol Pot time, my brothers learned to respond to hardship in very different ways. Meng often credits Pol Pot time with learning necessary survival skills. When a lake once separated him from a worksite, he learned to swim on his own.

We learned to hunt and set traps by stripping branches and stuff. We just taught ourselves how to make everything from the woods, like Rambo.

Pheng had different lessons. A sickly child who had scars inside his belly from being sick, Pheng learned how to appeal to others for help, and how to offer help whenever it was needed. Sometimes this appears to others as a weakness. But during times of hardship, it is the way we survive.

Pheng Troung and his family escaped from war-torn Cambodia in 1979 after be subjected to the horrors of the 'Khema Rouge' regime. Claiming refugee status, the family was brought to Canada in 1980. Now, some ten years after the ordeal, Pheng is finally able to tell his story. (Photo by Rob Bundy)

——Memories of Cambodia——

A survivor remembers the Killing Fields

A story by my brother, Pheng Troeung, on our escape from Cambodia.
"Memories of Cambodia: A survivor remembers the Killing Fields,"
printed in the Goderich Signal Star, *October 2, 1990.*

[beta]

On my brothers' 2021 visit to Vancouver, we pass a pet store, and they say the fish inside remind them of the camps. They joke about how, to survive the year of utter boredom at camp Khao-I-Dang, our family raised beta fish to fight each other. After sufficient training, my father would take the toughest of the bunch and bring them to the area where the Vietnamese soldiers lived, where they would fight to the death.

Though beta fish were certainly violent, they didn't quite satisfy my brothers' bloodlust. So, they began to raise crickets.

We put them in a shoebox with a little paper divider. Then we get them used to their own territories. Then, lift the paper and let them have it out!

My brothers stop in the mall, overtaken by the memory. They laugh about how their crickets would tear each other's limbs off, how they would screech and bleed. And no matter how battered or limbless the surviving cricket was, it still swung triumphantly around the little shoebox, swanking around the new territory it had acquired.

[bus]

1995. I'm fifteen years old when I transfer to St. Michael Catholic High School in Stratford, Ontario. I don't quite recall why I do this, except that I believe I can reshape myself, let my old self vanish, all my history and my name. My first step is to introduce myself as Elaine.

The first to punish me for this is a group of three boys on the school bus who know I changed my name. They pick on me, replace my new name with racist names, and throw my things out the window—things I cherish like pens and notebooks. The bus ride from Goderich to Stratford takes two hours, every single day.

Eventually, I'm called into the principal's office. The bus driver is concerned, but I say nothing, in fear of reprisal.

At home, I tell my brothers. *You're not just going to yell at them, right?* I say.

The next day, my brothers wait at the bus stop where the boys get off. In front of everyone my oldest brother Meng says, *I'm going to knock your fucking teeth out of your skull and then when the dentist fixes it I'm going to knock them out all over again.*

Two of the kids are stunned speechless. The third finds the threat funny and laughs. My brother smacks him in the face and he runs off crying.

That evening, one of the kids' parents calls and asks to speak with my brothers face to face. Not knowing what to expect, my brothers go, fully prepared to find the police waiting for them. Instead, the boys' parents thank them for disciplining their children.

When the boys on the bus leave me alone, the girls come for me. They're far worse than the boys. They drag me out into the soccer field and surround me in a circle. They toss me around the circle like a ball bounced back and forth. Perhaps their cruelty is emboldened by knowing that my brothers would never dare accost them in the same way.

To this day, I still have difficulty stepping onto a bus. Elaine still survives, but only in answer to the question, *Can I get a name for your coffee?* In all other matters, she lies in wait.

[torch]

I hear my father in the kitchen, washing dishes. Doing so is meditative for him, a daily cleansing, a spa for the hands. He only uses the dishwasher to store pots and pans.

While scrubbing plates, my father starts telling a story about the two years when he lived with the Kuy Indigenous people. It was in a small village fifty kilometres outside the city of Kampong Thom known as Phum O Pou (ភូមិ អូរពជី). At the time, in the late 1960s, the Chinese Cambodian community and the Kuy worked together in the business of trading and selling rice wine.

My father describes his relationship with the Kuy with great fondness. From the Kuy, my father learned how to survive in the wild: how to hunt, fish, work, and live off everything the forest could provide. He learned how to make medicinal remedies from resin and how to forage for food. Without this knowledge, my father often says, he might not have survived the harsh conditions of Pol Pot time, when Cambodian people were thrust into the jungles and forced to fend for themselves.

During Pol Pot time, my father tells us, a Kuy man even saved his life. Recognizing my father from *the old days*, the man helped conceal my father's identity from the Khmer Rouge cadres in the village. He gave my father two traditional torches made of dry preal leaves and rubber to help him navigate through the dark forest. The man bowed his hands in the gesture of the sampeah and said the torches were a gift to repay a debt from the past, when my father had been in good relations with the Kuy people.

I want to ask my father more about this, but I don't know if I have the words for it. I don't know if my father would even know what the word *Indigenous* means, let alone the politics, social lives, and histories that the term carries with it. I've read about how, during the Cold War, Cambodian Indigenous groups were recruited to fight on different sides of the war, and after the war, they either lived off its salvages or became soldiers in other lands.

My father takes a rag to a washed plate, making small circles across its hard surface. The dishes are done.

[pigeon]

On a hot summer day just after dinner, my son plays with his number toys while my husband Chris sits typing on his computer. I eat slowly, and am still mixing more of my father's chili garlic with the fried rice on my plate. In that brief and rare lull, my father tells a story about five pigeons.

He was at work one day taping trailer homes at his factory near Goderich, and one of his co-workers who owned a farm asked him, *Hey, do you want to buy a pigeon?*

A pigeon, a live one?

Yeah.

My father had eaten pigeons before, at a restaurant in Cambodia. Fried pigeons with beer. But he had never killed one himself.

How much?

Five dollars.

Oh pretty good. Okay, you bring me five tomorrow.

The next day, my father brought home five pigeons, all thumping around inside a little cardboard box. I was only ten years old and was frightened of the shaking box. *What is that?*

Pigeons.

What are you going to do with them?

Well, cook it. Eat.

Noooo! I screamed. My father tells me I looked scared.

Well, people eat it!

Noooo!!! I cried and cried. My father didn't want me to be sad, so he opened the box and let them all go. I was happy after that.

My husband, my father, my son, and I all share a laugh. I've heard this story countless times. It's the story my father always tells to describe my childhood. *Y-Dang was so sensitive*, my father says. *She never wanted anyone to get hurt, even pigeons!*

But that's not the end of the story. After another brief lull, my father continues. *Something happened a few days later. We went to a restaurant for a birthday party, all five of our family members in a car.*

And me? my son interjects.

You weren't born yet, my husband says from his computer.

Then why you say five people?

Well, my father says. *Two sons, one daughter, and mother and a father. That's five.*

Oh.

My father continues. It was winter, and after the party it was snowing, a heavy snow that covered everything. The car slipped to the side. He turned the wheel to the right and got stuck in a ditch. If he had turned to the left, *bam!* He would have collided into another car. Then, when the whole family got out to see the damage, another car passed by and nearly killed us.

The whole family, your brothers, your mother, and you, all got out of the car and pushed it out of the ditch. I said, good thing you made me let go of those five pigeons! There was one to save each of us!

We laugh again. My husband goes back to his typing, my son to his toys. I can't help but wonder if this birthday party was real. Perhaps it was. But all my memories of driving through snow-storms end with me waking up on the carpet in my mother's lap in a room full of Laotian, Cambodian, and Vietnamese refugees who are chewing tobacco, spitting out betel nuts, and playing cards next to garbage cans full of beer bottles. This often happened on long weekends, and sometimes, on Christmas Day.

I am about to put away the dinner's leftovers, but my father continues. *What you do is what you get*, he says in English, then in Khmer. *Te back bun back*. He goes on. *During Pol Pot, many people came back and saved my life. If just one person said one word during Pol Pot, I die.*

Who died? my son asks.

Your Grandpa, my father says. *They said nothing. Instead, they come and help me.*

And then you come alive again? my son says.

Yeah. Until today.

We laugh, though not as fully as before. Again, my father continues: *One time they sent me to the workplace, and I saw someone I knew. I was so happy to see him, and we talked about our past. We went to school together and played basketball together. Eventually, he became a policeman. "Where are you living now?" I asked. He told me. "And you?" I told him. At that time, we could not cross villages. The last thing he said to me was Don't tell anyone we know each other from before. Pol Pot hadn't found out yet that he worked for the police.*

We sit in silence. Even my son knows not to interrupt. Part of me wishes for the story to end. The pigeons were set free, we sur-vived. *Te back bun back*. The end. But the end never comes.

My father continues. *Not long after I came back to my village, I heard my old friend had been taken by the Khmer Rouge. Died. They found out he was a policeman. Thankfully, they didn't take his wife. So I found his wife. She said one day the Khmer Rouge came with a note telling him to bring a cow back from the fields. He seemed happy to do it. She waited days for him to come home. But that's it. Gone.*

He never gave up your name, I say.

Yeah.

He was tortured and he never gave you up.

Yeah.

I hear my husband typing, then talking to my son. I sit with my father in silence. I don't know what to do with these stories that go on and on. Why must a story about pigeons turn into a story about our family nearly dying in the snow to Pol Pot time to torture and death? My parents once thought I was blessed because I had spared some pigeons. *Te back bun back. Save a life, receive a life.* I repeat this to myself, just as my father does.

Te back bun back. Save a life, receive a life.

We honour those who helped us.

Te back bun back. Save a life, receive a life.

This is not gratitude. It is a passing on. A memory.

Te back bun back. Save a life, receive a life.

We honour them with our love, and with every story we tell.

Dearest Kai,

Today, I imagine you turning fifteen years old. You are a teen-ager now. You are becoming free. Soon, you will drive, travel, find new adventures, and live fully in the world around you. I wish I could be there to show you the world. Even now, writing this from 2021, I know there are many things I love doing, but I will never do again. I will never step foot on an airplane again. I will never show my love with the energy and vivacity I once did. I will never go to a concert, or go out dancing, again. And yet, we still have fun together. When your father put granola on a salad I made, I told him, *I just died a little bit inside. More than I already am*. We laughed for so long!

I wonder what the world will be like when you turn fifteen. Doctors tell me I should not look that far ahead. Every round of chemo feels like the ticking of a clock that hovers over my head. How many rounds do I have in me?

If I can give any advice to you at fifteen, it is to learn to trust others, and to listen to the ways they show their anger, their shy-ness, their hurt, and their love.

As I write this, your father and I have learned all the ways our family and friends express their love. When we were at the hospital, we felt in free-fall. Now, the reality of my illness has flooded around us, and every hour feels like it's drawn from a well of time that will soon dry. Waters of exhaustion flood in, submerging us, and everything outside comes only in weak reverberations. Sinking, we feel too tired to swim, until we can only see the sunlight through miles of water above us. We feel we might drown.

In Cambodia, there are age-old myths and legends of heavenly dancers and spirits called Apsaras. In the old stories, these dancers were created within a vast and churning sea. From the harsh energies of the ocean, the Apsaras rose to the surface through bubbles of foam.

It feels like we have been immersed within this violent sea. But like the Apsaras, the people up there, those who love and care for us, come to us with bubbles of air. Sometimes your father and grandparents can swim up, grab air bubbles, and bring them back down. Sometimes people from the surface come down with their bubbles, giving us life, breath by breath, knowing that all we need to keep going is to just breathe. Each bubble has something different inside: numbers, scents, warmth, rice, colours. And sometimes the bubbles are just bubbles that bulb and bub and pop!

Now, we have so many people diving down to meet us, cradling their bubbles from the surface, and we no longer need to go up and down. We stay here, living upon the oxygen of others. We have so many people and so many bubbles that they fill our entire house! Here, even at the bottom of an ocean, we have all we need to keep breathing. Like the Apsaras, we can make a home within the sea.

When I was fifteen, I remember the uncles, aunties, cousins, and friends, always coming in and out of our house, giving us life and love. I often avoided them—immersing myself within a book in my room. It took me many years to appreciate this constant stream of loved ones. And though I dare not look too far ahead, know always that their love is my love too. I live on within you, within them, in every gift they bring.

love always,
your mom

[pass]

It's 2012, on a Saturday. I'm thirty-two years old, and I'm about to fly back to Hamilton to undertake my Ph.D. dissertation defence.

Just before I leave for the airport, I receive a call from one of my older brother Meng's best friends, telling me that he's been arrested. Monday is bail day and Wednesday is defence day.

I call my supervisor, Don, to ask if I can cancel. He tells me I can . . . but I cannot. He tells me not to throw away what I have been working toward for six years. He reassures me that this will pass, that all the work has been done and I just need to take the final step. He tells me that my external examiner, Viet Nguyen, was happy with my thesis—and we know how high his standards can be.

I tell my family this story in 2021, about how I was a hair's breadth away from quitting, but Don, who died in 2019, saved me that day. He told me that my defence was just a formality. That I already had it. That I was better than I believed I ever could be. And that my life could never be sealed off from my work. My life was already part of my work.

My niece Sophia adds to this story. She remembers the Friday when her father was arrested, and the police came knocking on her door to tell her that he would be released later that night. She was left alone all weekend at twelve years old. She waited days for him to come home, slowly realizing that he wasn't coming, and that the police must have known this, too. My niece remembers this as the day she began to distrust the police.

My brother Meng, her father, tells his version. That Friday, the police were following him all day, but waited until he was smoking in a parking lot alone. They never even questioned him, nor did they let him talk to his daughter. By Monday, he was released. Months later, all of his charges were dropped, but not before the local newspaper had printed the names of the arrested, providing a permanent online catalogue of the alleged Southeast Asian gangsters in the area, one that could easily be found by potential employers, love interests, or academic institutions.

It's good that I didn't give up graduate school for them, my family tells me. I nod, thinking I wasn't exaggerating—I really was a hair's breadth away from giving it all up. Not for them, but for me.

[ringers]

It is April 2017. I'm in Goderich with Chris and Maddie. I'm giving them, and my son (five months in the womb), the tour of the town! We stop for lunch at the Bedford Hotel and then for ice cream at Cravings. It has been almost twenty years since I've lived here, but the familiarity hits me. This place, Alice Munro Country, is still my home.

We go to the beach and drive down to the Cove. We walk the boardwalk and take pictures by the water. I show them the area behind the large beach rocks, my hideout, where I used to spend hours lying under the sun. We go to the cemetery and I remember the many nights I spent here as a child waiting alone in the car as my parents and brothers would spread out among the gravestones looking for worms. I take in the gothic sight of the cemetery in the daytime. Our feet crunch on the winding gravel path as we make our way among the dead.

I take Chris and Maddie to a café, and Chris tenses up when he overhears the small-town chatter. Raised in big cities, Chris has been on his guard since we arrived in Goderich. He hears someone say, *they must be out-of-townies*, and immediately wants to leave.

I tell him that this isn't necessarily an insult. I point to the sign on the door that says *refugees welcome* in both English and Arabic. Later on, we meet Syrian refugees who remind me of my own family, hosted by a different church. They even have a daughter who, like myself, would rather hide under the table than come to greet strange visitors.

We do a *ringer* around the town square, a walk that sounds circular but in fact traces an octagon. We stop at the library, where Maddie and I wander giddily through the stacks. We find no copies of Alice Munro's books, but we come across a few of Maddie's novels! She poses with a cover of *Dogs at the Perimeter*, a book that changed my life, a book that I return to for teaching, research, and literary companionship. *Dogs* was not the first of Maddie's novels I read, but it was the one that brought us together, made us "found sisters." Her companionship has been present in my life ever since, and she is one of the few writers I know who is devoted to telling the stories of migrants, refugees, and rebels without reducing their personhood.

I bring Chris and Maddie to the library's basement, the children's section, and I show them another one of my hideouts. I see myself as a young girl, encamped in the corner, reading books by Alice Munro. I hope one day the child in my womb will come here, and feel transported by books. He will read Munro and Maddie, but he will also find refuge in other stories.

[killing fields]

It's 2019 and I sit in my living room scrolling through photos on my phone of my recent trip to Cambodia while my son tries to grab it out of my hand. He looks at the screen and randomly recites the numbers he sees. *4:14!* he shouts gleefully. The August sunshine streams in through the window and my son rolls around on the soft carpet. Not yet two, my son has developed a fascination with numbers that amuses the whole family to no end. He is the centre of our lives now, the gravity that pulls us all together.

Chris walks into the room and peers over my shoulder at the photos. He is a good father, a good partner, a lifeline when I had none. I take him through a few photos. *This one is from the morning I took a tuk-tuk out to Choeung Ek*, I tell him. I didn't want to go, but felt I had to. So many people were talking about it at the conference. One woman, an American forensic expert, reported on her findings from exhuming and examining thousands of skulls. *Most died of blunt force trauma to the head*, I remember her saying, as she pointed to a large image of skulls projected onto her PowerPoint screen.

When I went to Choeung Ek this time, I tell Chris, *the nauseating feeling that welled up in my gut was the same. It always feels like the vibrations of the ground are rising up and coursing through me. Did you know it used to be a Chinese cemetery? That the mass graves used to crack open from the top in the early days, as if something was bubbling up from beneath?*

[stand]

The most famous monument at Choeung Ek is known to tourists as *the Killing Tree*. For many, it leaves an imprint on the mind of Cambodian babies thrashed against trees by the Khmer Rouge. And yet, I am holding my son in my arms as I show him this image of myself beside this tree.

In Maggie Nelson's *The Argonauts*, the Killing Tree is invoked as a synecdoche of horror, as the distinctly violent and barbaric menace that gives greater value to the white child's safety. Returning from her holiday, Nelson's mother comes away with only one lesson from her trip to the Killing Fields. Nothing about Cambodian loss or regeneration, but rather, a reaffirmation of what she, white mother, must fear and safeguard herself against.

Cambodia, a place of absolute savagery, a warning about what happens to babies *over there*. Nelson's mother cannot stop herself from retelling her tale. She needs her daughter to know that she stood before the tree, because the brave act of *standing before the tree* is more important than the tree itself.

Cambodia's tragedy is the background of human rights, and of motherhood. It is the parameter of unimaginable death. The children who died, suffered, and were debilitated during Pol Pot time are incidental, anecdotal, collateral.

I show my child the Killing Tree at Choeung Ek because I want him to know that his history is not just the raw material through which others can define themselves. I want him to know that events like this happened, continue to happen, and will happen again. For us, we do not fear death but imagine it always within our grasp. We stand near the Killing Tree not just to witness this history. We stand in solidarity with those who suffered there, and we stand to fight against its inevitable return.

[tree]

At Choeung Ek, I look down at the soil at the base of the Killing Tree. I ask another tourist to take a photo of me, feeling embarrassed but wanting a record of this moment.

I stand here as a mother now. I want my son to know about the Killing Tree. I want him to go there himself someday, unafraid. I will tell him, *it's not the outer parameter of horror, as some would say. It's where your grandmother and grandfather and your uncles came from. Your roots are here. Don't be afraid.*

"The Killing Tree" at Choeung Ek Genocidal Center, Cambodia.
Photo from Y-Dang Troeung.

[door]

Are you sure you want to walk through that door today? my therapist
asks me. He is referring to my desire to talk about my childhood
and especially my relationship with my mother. In past conversations, I have noted that some of these memories are just too
difficult for me to talk about. He asks me, *What's different about
today that makes you feel like you can go there?* I say that the fights
between me and my mother have been escalating, and with all of us
squeezed together in a two-bedroom home during the pandemic,
old patterns have begun to resurface. I also admit to him, with an
embarrassed chuckle, that I feel okay *going there* today because
I booked a 7 p.m. session rather than my usual daytime appoint-
ment. He laughs because he knows me so well. He knows that I am
so pragmatic, so focused on productivity, that I save the heaviest
baggage for days when I don't have anything to do after the ther-
apy session. If I bring up my mother during a morning session,
the whole day will be a writeoff. And I can't afford to waste a day.

Over the course of an hour, I walk through that door with him.

I am a young girl, curled up on the floor in my bedroom, quietly crying. I lean against my bedroom door, holding it closed.

Me joa!!, meaning, *worthless daughter, piece of trash*. These and other names signal the beginning of another long rant.

I ask myself why as tears stream down my face. It feels like an eternity. I don't even know what she is saying anymore. I just know that she has snapped into one of her episodes and there is nothing I can do but wait out the storm. Her words are a rainstorm in a ravine, and the door is my only protection from the torrent. I know that no one will come to comfort me or rescue me, not my father, who is numbed in these moments, not my brothers, who are never home or are too scared to intervene.

Before I know it, my therapist snaps me out of it. Maybe I have walked too far. He has grabbed my hand and is leading me out of that room. My relationship with my mother, the feelings of emotional abandonment by my father who did nothing—all these things are too much to take on in one day. For now, I need to be gently led out the door.

[repeat]

It is already August, many months into my cancer diagnosis, and I apologize to my therapist profusely for not making time for any sessions. I feel bad that I have only spoken to him twice since the diagnosis last year. I explain that I have been in bare survival mode, my days full of chemotherapy infusions, blood work, blood transfusions, fluid drains, doctors' appointments, nurse visits, nutrition appointments, physiotherapy, CT scans, X-rays, and on and on. When I am not at the hospital or cancer centre, I am exhausted, barely able to get up some days or even speak from bed. He says, so kindly, so gently, *You don't owe anything to this space. There's nothing to apologize for.*

What brings me here today, I say in response to his usual opening query, is that, number one, I have been feeling stronger these past few weeks due to a new chemotherapy regimen that seems to finally be working. At the same time, my new strength has been tinged by the distress of having to pay out of my own pocket for my own treatment. All my renewed energies have been spent galvanizing friends and colleagues to write letters to the health minister, to the insurance company, to the pharmaceutical company, and to my university's administration. The medical industry has granted me more time, only to sap it all away in bureaucratic slow death. And this new layer of financial burden has broken not only me, but those in my home.

I explain that a terrible scene unfolded the other night. A fight between me and my mother devolved into a state of madness. It was the same old scene except, this time, intensified by my mother's difficulty in coping with my cancer.

I tell him that I think the cancer of a loved one must bring out the best and the worst in people, that they can either rise to the situation with unexpected compassion and care, or they can't cope, and the cruellest sides of their personalities emerge. I have experienced it. Some loved ones have come closer, reaching out with the most unexpected tenderness, love, and commitment. Others have "ghosted," distanced themselves, or lashed out.

From my mother, in the wake of my cancer, I have seen both sides emerge. I have seen her silent devotion and love like at no other time in my life, picking up my fallen hair from the bathroom floor, cutting up fruit and bringing it to my bedside, praying for me at the temple, washing my clothes night after night, and bathing my son when I or my husband are too exhausted to do so. But on other nights, her anger has erupted with an intense, pent-up fury. On these days, I feel as though my cancer, and the burdens that have come with it, has become a disease that has poisoned not just me, but everyone around me.

Living within Cambodian and Chinese culture, it is me, the daughter, who takes care of her elderly parents. I worked tirelessly to pay off their mortgage, and prided myself on finding them housing in Vancouver, first in our home and then in a nearby studio.

I spent years making us a stronger family unit so we could create new memories together.

I explain to my therapist that my growing anguish resides not just in my inability to be a dutiful daughter for my parents, but in my growing inability to be a mother to Kai, and to protect him from the darkest moments of the childhood that I had. The other night, Kai witnessed an epic fight between my mother and me. It was the kind of argument we have had hundreds of times. But these days, these fights unfold as soon as my husband, my father, or my brothers have just left to run an errand. This time, for the first time in his life, my son was there to witness it. He watched as my mother and I raged against each other, our screams built up over decades of unresolved misunderstanding.

Kai begged us to stop fighting, saying over and over, *too loud!* I knew it wasn't just his sensitivity to noise because when I said *Mom, lower your voice, the neighbours will call the police!* and my mother said *fine call the police, I don't care, call the police!* Kai ran into his bedroom screaming *noooooooooo*, drowning out the sounds of us both.

I joined my son in his room, where he begged me to read him a book so we would stop fighting. *Please Mama*, he said, *read me the* Good Night Toronto *book*. Another one, *Dear Zoo*. Another one, *No! My First Book of Protest*. In this moment, barricaded in my son's bedroom with his books and the music I had cranked up to max to drown out my mother's shrieks, I was transported back to my own childhood, when I was the child on the other side of the door.

Through tears, I tell my therapist that I know all children witness fights between adults, but I also know from experience that this imprint never leaves. It grows, infects your memory, your focus, and your future. I wanted so badly to protect my son from this, to give him a childhood without the screams and the threats. It broke my heart when Kai said to me afterwards, *Why is grandma so mean to Mama?*

What we say to children in these moments is really important, my therapist tells me. What I wanted to say to Kai was please forgive your grandma, for she has been through enough pain for a dozen lifetimes, and it has taken root deep within her. Seeing her daughter in pain has driven her to the edge, because she feels helpless to lessen my suffering, to stop the illness growing inside of me. I want to tell him that his grandmother has felt this way before, for four years when she could not feed her own children, and when she was pregnant with me and there were no doctors or hospitals left. Wars and their aftermaths turn the world upside down, turn parents into children and children into parents. I had to be an adult well before my time, but I don't want this for my son.

My son is too young to understand these things for now. All I was able to say that night was, *I'm so sorry*.

My therapist says, Let me reframe this scene a little for you. It sounds like you were the adult in this moment, not Kai. It sounds like he was a child reacting to a stressful situation, not consciously trying to defuse a fight. It was you who took him out of the conflict, comforted him, put the music on, and read him his books. *Did anyone ever do that for you when you were a child? What if someone, an adult, had been there to do that for you?*

[boneyards]

It is July 2018. Today is the last day of my visit to Siem Reap. Later this afternoon I have to catch my flight, and the thought of being so far away from Cambodia pains me deeply. I have failed to do so much: six years ago I moved to Asia to take a job as a professor, and to be closer to Cambodia. I longed for proximity to my parents' birthplace—to see with my own eyes the landscapes of their past. I hoped to lay down some kind of record of the war they had survived, to write a book that my mother and father and brothers could see themselves in. But many things in Cambodia have taken me by surprise; it is one thing to inherit the shadows of the past, another to walk among them.

I arrive at the War Museum Cambodia, just outside Siem Reap, about five kilometres south of the ancient ruins of Angkor Wat. In the sweltering afternoon heat, I take in the arresting sight of the fenced-in outdoor space: dozens of obsolete war machines are interspersed among the banyan and palm trees. At a glance, the rusted brown tanks and aircraft carriers merge seamlessly with the browns of the trees, soil, and pits. The remains of war are starting to be reclaimed by nature. Lifeworlds woven together. Unlike the nearby ruins of the ancient Angkor empire, an attraction that draws millions of tourists each year, this boneyard feels hidden from the world.

Inside the museum, I learn that war material in Cambodia used to be scrapped for recycled metal. People salvaged what they could to make a living. I spent time in graveyards as a child, alone in the car at night as my family members scavenged the ground for earthworms they could sell to farmers. Back then, I grew excited watching my parents move among the dead, but today I feel unsure of how to move through such a ghostly area.

[art]

In the War Museum Cambodia compound, one caption catches my eye: "Artillery 85 mm made in China, 1946. 4.75 m length, size 85 mm, fighting power approximately 13.10 km, was used in Cambodia by Pol Pot regime (1975–1979) and was finally destroyed in 1998 at Osmach battlefield the West of Siem Reap Province."

This retired artillery is a fragment of a missing picture: one of fraternity between China and Cambodia—brothers in arms, some would say. This is an image of Cambodia that most have preferred not to see, drawn instead to the iconic pictures of skulls and bones, of the sunken earth of mass graves. Many tourists have gaped at the horrors of Pol Pot's Killing Fields, have shaken their heads in astonishment at the sheer brutality of this regime, but few have cared to see the horrors committed before and after Pol Pot's time: the military aid that flowed from China to the Khmer Rouge, the bombs that the United States dropped on Cambodia, the refugees who were turned back at the borders.

One exhibit, labelled "Bomb House," gives an account of these bombs. The exhibit makes it clear that this boneyard is a cemetery of the *longue durée* of imperial violence in Cambodia.

This land houses the remnants of one of the hottest laboratories of the Cold War, where the US secretly dropped more than 2.7 million tons of bombs, more bombs than the Allies dropped in all of World War II combined.

The Bomb House is a wooden hut whose walls are lined with deactivated rockets. An information board displays an archival photo of Richard Nixon pointing at a map of Cambodia. Here stands a technician, the man who turned Cambodia into an experiment in "collateral damage." My mother and father's stories about fleeing from the US bombs suddenly come back to me. *To hide from the American bombs, we took shelter under a Buddhist pagoda*, my father once told me. I recall their stories of how, when the Khmer Rouge rose to power in the ashes of US bombs, my parents and brothers slept in the fields for almost four years, barely clinging to life. In the hazy afternoon heat, I feel the familiar emotions of anger and bitterness rise in me.

[cat]

The museum's winding dirt paths cut around inert weapons, creating a maze for solo travellers and tour groups looking for their fix of the war-ravaged exotic. Cambodian men dressed in blue army uniforms, likely former Khmer Rouge soldiers, offer tours of the surroundings. Many guides carry the wounds of war—prosthetics, bullet wounds, and scars—visible for all to see.

One guide assembles me and a small group of English-speaking visitors. He tells us: *I spent nearly my whole life in the war. I died more than ten times during the war. They called me a cat. I will show you the scar, the shrapnel, the ball bearing. Everywhere there are holes in my body.*

At one point during his story, a thirty-something American man in the group, on break from his conference in Chiang Mai, leans over and asks me if I know who Pol Pot is. I have no time for explanations today.

Head & Power *(2018) by Svay Sareth. The head is stuffed with kapok fibres, symbolizing the muting effects of authoritarianism. Courtesy of the artist.*

[mine]

Our guide at War Museum Cambodia says: *They took away my family and then they killed them. I ate the crickets, grasshoppers, frog, fish, snake, everything. A hornet's nest dropped down on me. I live thirty miles north from here. About fifty kilometres. My wife died three years ago. Lung cancer from the uranium. On April 16, 2017, my friend stepped on a mine and it took off his legs.* He takes us to a large ruined tank and peers over the top to point out something inside: *My friend's bones inside. Bowin. He died.*

I feel a whirling as I listen to him, wishing he would stop, but I am incapable of extracting myself from the group. I'm jolted out of my daze as our guide ends his monologue to ask our names. I tell him mine, and there is immediate recognition on his part: *You were born in Khao-I-Dang! Khao-I-Dang is the mountain in Thailand. Her name,* he says to the group, *is the same as that mountain. Some, like your family, when they went to Thailand, were very, very lucky. They got to immigrate, to live in Canada, Australia, New Zealand, the US, and Europe, but some were not so lucky. They got repatriated by the United Nations. I see that you are a little bit upset, but you will know how lucky you are.*

I don't know how to respond, to express the sadness I feel in this moment, standing before this man whom I should call *bou* ("uncle" in Khmer) but don't. Uncle, I want to say, I'm sorry your life has been so hard.

An Australian woman, with two bored and indifferent teenage daughters, jumps in: *Yes, we are very lucky to be Australian, but we have a lot of different cultures that like to bring their cultures into Australia*—laughter from the group—*which is actually the dangerous part.*

Our group passes by Chinese-speaking tourists who pose for photos with old rifles and tanks, as if wishing the equipment could be suddenly reanimated. The captions are all in English. More than once a Chinese-speaking passerby stops me, points at something, and asks me in Putonghua, *Zhè shì shénme* (这是什么)—*What is this?* I shrug and say, *Wǒ bù zhīdào* (我不知道)—*I don't know.*

[bloom]

There is a crater at the edge of the War Museum Cambodia compound that is fenced in by razor wire but curiously unmarked. Our
guide tells us it was caused by the US bombing in 1973, but there is
noticeable hesitation in his voice. He doesn't want to linger here,
quickly moving us on to the next station.

I wonder what in the museum is real and what is fabricated, if
it even matters. At the centre of the crater, a little ecosystem has
formed, with bright-pink lotus blossoms sprouting up from a pool
of lily pads and murky brown water. The Cambodian belief is that
the lotus flower emerging from the mud symbolizes strength, hope,
faith that a new lifeworld can be reborn from the darkest places.
I think of the biology of cellular and organic regrowth—that
every species, no matter how damaged, is capable of regeneration.

The blazing sun shines in my eyes and time has gotten away from
me. Something has both paralyzed me and left me ungrounded.
When I arrive at Siem Reap airport, I find I have missed my flight.

A lotus pond grows in the space of a former bomb crater, either real or fabricated.
War Museum Cambodia, Siem Reap, 2018. Photo by Y-Dang Troeung.

[pain]

I tell my therapist about my pain. He always wants to think through metaphors, to think of my pain like a mountain, an ocean, a colour, a void. No, I want to talk about pain: physical, present, manifesting, corporeal *pain*.

Pain: feeling like my organs want to fall out of my body; it feels like the cancer has infiltrated my bones; it feels like something is moving around or beating or pulsing in my stomach and liver and it causes me rivers of pain.

My pain is unrelenting. It throbs at my right side—a good thing, I am told, because my left side contains my heart. My pain is manifest of what's deeper inside—not a history or a memory or an idea, but a cluster of tumours. My pain is undeniable. On days when I feel like I may live through this still, the pain responds, *no*.

Many people believe pain is an incident, like feeling a pinch or a slap or a punch. My pain is not like this. It can't be compared to anything merely physical like a wound or a scar, nor anything merely psychological, the pain of loss, nor any existential pain, the pain of rolling around at night, sleeping only an hour or two or not at all.

Pain is when lying down, sitting, standing, walking, are all deeply uncomfortable. Pain is when there is no position for relaxation, no way to get relief. Just endless moving from one thing to another and no amount of medication can bring a release.

This is pain as being, pain as personhood, just as being a refugee has been my personhood. Pain is fearing the night because I always know what will happen to me throughout the night. Pain is feeling totally normal, but then seeing myself in the mirror shaking and crying and wishing I was in a different plane of existence and realizing that my normalcy is shaking and crying and wishing I was in a different plane of existence.

Pain is when you try to do anything you can to stop the pain. Pain is the way my head sags downward and can't seem to feel comfortable upright. Pain is blaming myself for my own pain. Pain is feeling so guilty about making my loved ones deal with my pain that I try as hard as I can to conceal my pain in front of them. Pain is seeing the stunned, pale expressions on the faces of my husband, my son, my mother, or my father, and knowing that my pain is causing them pain. Should I feel bad for having pain?

Nothing here should be what it is, my therapist says.

Pain is realizing that I may live with this pain forever, and in that same moment, knowing that I can't live with this pain forever.

My therapist asks for a moment when I felt I could see my pain, when I had control over it.

I remember a time. On the week of my diagnosis, a friend came to my hospital room. Her mother had died just months before, from a tumour in her brain. But it was not the tumour per se that killed her. It was MAID: Canada's medical assistance in dying program.

My friend shows me pictures of her mother just minutes before the lethal injection. *It's a really weird picture*, my friend says. But it is not weird to me. Her mother looks happy, radiant, surrounded by family who sit next to her holding her arms.

What was your mother like? I ask her. After a moment, my friend responds, *She was the kind of woman who would polish her nails while driving*.

For a moment, I feel outside my pain. In my mind, I can smell the polish and hear the road.

Dearest Kai,

I am writing this during another long hospital stay. In this time of distress and uncertainty, my strength for survival has been built upon those around me. My family, and you. But I want to write to you about your father, who has been by my side through so many difficult times and has devoted all of his being to care for me.

Since the day we met, your father and I have had a connection that I can only describe as cosmic. We met at a conference soon after graduate school, when we had both taken jobs in Asia, and were searching for a home far outside our given homes. We both chose to live alone in a country whose language we could only partially speak. The day we met in Hong Kong, I was totally in love, and with such complete certainty that it was startling (and even a bit frightening!). After just a few days we decided to be together. I was feverishly happy and in a daze, and I wanted the future to stretch on forever with him in it.

His family came from mixed Chinese and Filipino plantation workers, mine from mixed Chinese and Cambodian merchants. Both our families lived through migration and poverty. We both had ancestors who had fled conscription, colonialism, and war. For both of us, travel across Asia was not an excursion or joyride. It was a way to connect to the lands and peoples who, like our families, had undergone damage and loss. His interest in all these countries he went to, Myanmar, Indonesia, Malaysia, came from a burning desire to understand their relations to each other, and to himself.

When we met, neither of us had ever planned to get married. We just knew. There was no one else like him, like me, like us. We were instantly a couple, engaged a year later, married a year after that, and the next year, we had you. People described us as fast-moving, as "the lovebirds." We loved in a blaze, as if we knew we wouldn't have enough time. And the pulse of Hong Kong gave a beat to our romance. We were always moving, always changing, but we always flowed together.

Our romance constantly brought us back to Phnom Penh, where we danced to 1960s rock and roll music the way your grandparents did. While they grooved in dance halls, we bounced in nightclubs. While they went around on motorbikes, we sat spooning in the back of tuk-tuks. I remember circling the Independence Monument, a memorial to Cambodia's independence from France, my head on your father's chest, watching the golden streetlights whiz by.

We called each other soulmate from the first month we were together, and it is in the comfort of this word, *soulmate*, that we felt our spirits wed. During our marriage ceremony, we gave this word more meaning when we tied red thread around our wrists, a Khmer symbol of the eternal binding of souls. Even past this life, we would find each other again.

You & I, *drawn by hand with black ink pen and digitally coloured (2017).*
Artwork by Visothkakvei. Courtesy of the artist.

One ceremony wasn't enough. Our love was so overflowing that we had another marriage in Hawai'i, near your father's family, on Waimānalo Beach.

Though I loved your father in an instant, I knew I would marry him when I came to admire his talents. Boy, does he have talents! From early in our relationship, I knew that his mind worked differently than others'. He can always take in more thoughts, embrace more ideas, and focus so sharply that only when he's finished with his task at hand will he look up and realize I've rearranged the entire room! What he doesn't say, his mind will speak beautifully through his writing. One day you may find monuments of his love for me in his novels, short stories, and poems, which are so often about love, and about us. He has the same beautiful mind that I see in you, when you play with your numbers or letters and your mind races with knowledge, when I see you learning new skills all on your own, and when I see your joy in solving puzzles that other children would find tedious. You both share that talent of being able to discover fun in just about anything. I am happy knowing that you two will not be strangers to each other, that you will always share this connection.

In these difficult times, I have come to rely more and more on your father's persistence, his ability to stay calm in terrible situations. Like me, your father has endured many hardships, so much that he has never known what it means to be firmly settled in a place. He seems to feel at home in hardship, and his endurance has gotten us through the worst moments of my diagnosis. Despite the misery of this disease, your father has always reminded me that it has brought us closer together, and that he feels fortunate to spend all day by my side in my hospital room, holding my hand, telling jokes, massaging my legs when I feel pain, and helping me exercise when I have energy, leaving my side only to attend to you. The nurses tell us that we are the cutest couple in the hospital, and that even though we have been married for six years now, we still act like newlyweds! He brings anything I ask to my hospital room: pillows, blankets, clothes, stuffed animals, furniture, books. And every morning he appears with a breakfast of my choosing! He has brought so many things from our house, that now even this sterile hospital room feels like a new home.

I know that, whatever happens to me, you will be in good hands, with a father who will always be your companion. There may be times when you need him, and he needs you. I know he will carry some guilt when I am gone, and I fear that my disease will change him, as it may change you. I hope you both will not be afraid to turn this tragedy into something you can talk about, even laugh about. Like your father, perhaps you will find ways to inhabit hardship, to transform it from something resembling death to something that can give life, just as you have both been life-giving forces for me.

I hope, too, that you can be free in the world, just as we were. Find love and hope wherever you can, just as your grandparents did. Your father and I had no home until we found each other. Know that, wherever you are, our home and the love we share within it will be with you always.

love you,
your mom

[montreal uncle]

When we arrived in Canada as refugees in 1980, my extended family was scattered all across the world. One node of the Troeung family went to live in a small town in southwestern Ontario, sponsored by a private church group; another node went to Hull, Quebec, and then later settled in Montreal; others went to Australia to live near Sydney; others to Paris. We, the node who went to Ontario, were closest to our Montreal node, and as a family, we made frequent summer excursions to Quebec, where there seemed to be a boundless number of cousins and aunties and uncles to whom I was told I was related, though I could never figure out exactly how.

I remember asking my father about one of my uncles in Montreal who always fascinated me, with his gangster-like swagger and his dark sunglasses. We called him Montreal Uncle, and Montreal Uncle had been blinded in one eye ever since Pol Pot time when he was sent to a Khmer Rouge labour camp. One day, when he was chopping wood at this camp, a sharp wood chip flew up and pierced his eye. As there was no medicine or treatment available during this time, his maimed eye became infected, and he eventually lost vision in that eye.

Though he managed to survive the genocide and resettle in Canada as a refugee, Montreal Uncle's health remained fragile throughout his life. He suffered from diabetes, frequent bouts of fainting, mental disorientation, and mobility impairment. He was often misdiagnosed by doctors and prescribed the wrong kind of medication. At times, he spoke in hallucinatory fragments, confused about where he was and who he was with.

After one particularly bad collapse in his home, a hospital MRI brain scan revealed that Montreal Uncle had suffered a stroke at some point in his life. He had been living for years, maybe even decades, in a state of *post-rupture*, to use the language of stroke medicine, that had gone undetected and untreated.

Montreal Uncle passed in October 2021, from what I would later find out to be pancreatic cancer. Until then, I never knew if anyone else in my family had experienced this disease.

[texas uncle]

The story of Montreal Uncle has captivated me for many reasons besides his health, as I knew he was the father of another uncle of mine, whom we always refer to today as Texas Uncle.

Texas Uncle was a son of Montreal Uncle's first marriage, to a Vietnamese woman in Cambodia in the late 1960s. When the Vietnamese ethnic community started becoming targets of the Lon Nol dictatorship in the early 1970s, Texas Uncle's mother packed up her baby son and fled to Vietnam, where they lived until she died one day from a poisonous snakebite while working in the fields.

When the border to Cambodia reopened in 1979, Texas Uncle, then a teenager on his own, wandered back to a destroyed Cambodia in search of his biological father. By this time, however, his father was already in Montreal. Their separation would continue for a few more years until Montreal Uncle, a highly resourceful man, managed to secure his son's sponsorship to Canada. Texas Uncle arrived in Canada as a young man in his twenties, along with a family of his own (a wife and two *paper daughters*) that had been reconstructed in the refugee camp.

For years after their reunion in Canada, Montreal Uncle and Texas Uncle, father and son, found some semblance of peace and normalcy in their lives, despite Montreal Uncle's frequent health problems. Together, the pair opened up a small convenience store in a rough neighbourhood of Montreal that soon became a frequent target for robberies. Eventually, everyone in the family who sometimes helped out in the store, including the kids, my cousins, got used to robberies and violence as a reality of their everyday lives.

One day, tragedy struck: an armed robber entered the convenience store and shot Texas Uncle in the stomach before fleeing with the contents of the cash register. Although Texas Uncle recovered from his wounds, he no longer felt at ease in Montreal. He felt nervous and anxious at every turn while walking its streets. It was no longer his home, if it ever had been.

Hearing rumours about Cambodian American refugees who were making it big by opening donut shops and franchises in Houston, Texas Uncle crossed the forty-ninth parallel and once again transitioned into a new life.

[cousin]

Just before Montreal Uncle died, his son, my cousin, flew from Montreal to visit me in Vancouver, bringing a charming young girlfriend of Vietnamese and Chinese descent. He is Cambodian, she is Vietnamese. In the new diaspora, the old hatreds seem to have faded.

Perhaps because he knows what I do for a living, my cousin asks me many questions about Pol Pot time, about our family's experience in the war, and their struggles in Canada. I ask why he doesn't already know all this.

My dad just never liked to talk about that time. He doesn't talk much period.

We talk throughout the trip, his girlfriend attentively listening as I retell the stories of our family in my own way. We talk as we walk down the beach, as we leaf through pictures of our family, and between Chinese karaoke songs.

Finally, he asks, *Why did my dad go to Montreal? Why did we not join you all in Ontario? We could have been a bigger family.*

I tell him I cannot know the answer to this, though it seems like one of many family secrets.

[deport]

I often think of the men in my family, my uncles, father, and brothers. They are male refugees who do not strike gratitude in the hearts of most people they pass, but fear, and sometimes anger. I have witnessed how these men spend their lives gripped by the constant fears of violence, unemployment, incarceration, and in some cases deportation.

December 2013, I am sitting down for an interview in Phnom Penh with the Cambodian American deportee and spoken word poet Kosal Khiev, whose case has become emblematic in a deportation crisis that appears to have no end in sight.

We share a common point of intersection in our past. Like many "1.5 generation" Cambodian refugees in the diaspora, Kosal and I were both born in 1980 in Khao-I-Dang refugee camp, my namesake. Our families were both part of the nearly one million refugees who fled from the Khmer Rouge to the border of Thailand in hopes of being resettled in the West. While Kosal and his family were part of the 100,000 Cambodian refugees who went to the United States, my family and I were part of the 20,000 who went to Canada. We are now part of the refugee returnees with one major difference: my return to Cambodia is voluntary; his is not.

The word *deportation* derives from the Middle French as *a carrying away from one country to another or to a distant place; to carry off, transport, banish, exile*. Deportation and imprisonment are similar to being a refugee fleeing war, in that we are forever defined by the moment we were carried from one space into another. In time, we are meant to forget who we once were.

Our interview is candid; Kosal is shirtless, and I am trying to remain professional. We joke but return again and again to politics. Outside, in the streets of Phnom Penh, there have been daily demonstrations led by the opposition Cambodia National Rescue Party (CNRP), who are seeking to force Prime Minister Hun Sen to step down following disputed election polls. International news has said that the protestors number up to 500,000, many of whom are young activists as well as striking garment workers.

The next day, military police fire on protestors, murdering four people and forcing an end to the labour strikes. I am not there to witness this. I have left Phnom Penh, and watch these events on the news. Afterwards, I realize I have somehow lost my interview with Kosal. I look through every folder of my laptop, but nothing remains of the words we shared—gone to history, deleted.

[ring]

While visiting us in Vancouver, my cousin from Montreal takes a two-day trip to Whistler with his girlfriend. When they return, she is his fiancée.

My cousin proposed at the top of a mountain. We flip through his phone's many pictures attempting to capture the event—none of them *Instagram-worthy*, but that's just fine.

I feel glad to be the first person in the family to see these pictures, to talk to my cousin and his new fiancée face to face about their decision. I am the first to see the joy and hope in their eyes, and I feel a deep love for them, and for this moment.

We promise we will meet them in Montreal for their wedding. I can't wait to see them tie the red knots around their wrists, tethering their souls together. I imagine that we will be there, and we will bring our families with us, and we will reunite with our uncles, and our scattered cousins and aunties and nieces and nephews. We will be there, I pray, even if it's snowing.

Dearest Kai,

Today is the day you graduate high school—or perhaps you
dropped out. Mama loves you either way.

For most of my life my dream has been to teach young people
around your age how to think and, more importantly, how to
live, despite all the thinking. I know you might feel like so much
depends on grades, on keeping busy, on proving yourself above
the people around you, even those you call your friends. You are
entering a world whose main ambition is to separate you from
others, to make you compete and fight and demean each other for
scraps. Do not lose heart, and be kind to those whose only understanding of living and loving is to wrestle others into the mud.

The first thing I did when I was diagnosed with this illness
was look over my calendar and balk at all the things I had sched-
uled to do later that week. I was to attend a writing workshop
with a known scholar. I was to host an interview. I was to both
manage and speak at a virtual event. I was to mark dozens of
mid-term papers. I was to try and finish a chapter of a book
that I had been delaying for nearly a year due to the stress of

constantly thinking about the book itself. This, all on top of teaching, committee meetings, shopping, mothering, and taking care of your grandparents.

Terrible as this illness is, it has also relieved me of all the things I thought I had to do, all the things about being a professional academic that I believed I had failed to achieve. I don't have to do any of these things anymore, and besides, these things never had anything to do with keeping my job, or being able to provide for my family, or my health. I look at my past life and it looks back at me and we both envy each other. I envy her mental and physical health, her capacity to do so much; she envies my debility, which allows me to do the bare minimum, to focus and to be present with my family and friends and to live every day with a heart full of love.

At this point in your life, you may feel swayed by different religious and spiritual guidance. Perhaps this has become more important due to my own absence from your life. Though you may not identify as a refugee yourself, remember how we are trees without roots, cut off from an assured and practical knowledge of cultural traditions. Death for us has no given ritual. We don't know how to accept a friend's well-wishes without also expecting more from them. When it comes to major life events, we don't know what we should be doing, who to pray to, how to dress, when to go through the motions or even what those motions should be.

Though I once went to Catholic school and though you may remember me praying to the many Chinese gods, my religion is and always has been knowledge itself. But to believe in knowledge is to put your faith in your own mental abilities to determine the best path forward. To believe in knowledge is to trust the capacities of your own mind. But the burden of this, as I have come to find, takes its toll.

In your own race after graduation, you may seek to become part of the class of citizens who accomplish many things. I was that person, but I have lost the privilege of accomplishment. For the past two years at least, I have been in a time of need, but I have slowly learned to do less, and to ask for help. There are times to work, and there are times to let others take on those tasks. One day, the many, many tasks you see before you will no longer be your concern.

love always,
your mom

[mute]

Cambodians have a phrase to describe the loss of language in Pol Pot time. It is *dam-doeum-kor*, which translates to *planting the kapok tree* or *mute tree*. The emphasis on *planting* and *rooting* suggests that when language abandoned us, when words were no longer capable of making meaning of our world, Cambodians still nurtured the seed of rebirth and regeneration, believing that, from the void within, the kapok tree would one day re-emerge. Silence during Pol Pot time carried an intentionality, a planting of something for an imagined future that was not yet visible.

In the case of many Cambodian women like my mother, this seed was a physical human life itself, nurtured in the womb and long afterwards. The kapok tree, the refugee child who would one day speak for herself, is like the lotus flower that grows out of the mud. It symbolizes the capacity for the renewal of life, for rebirth of spirit and *pralung* (soul) in the darkest places.

A kapok tree swaying in the field in the countryside in Cambodia.
Photo by The camvalleys, via Shutterstock.

Harvested kapok tree fibres, Kampong Cham Province, August 28, 2016.
Screen capture from "Kapok in Cambodia" by Leanghort Sok (via YouTube).

[kapok]

When I was growing up, my father often told me about the kapok tree. As a child, he loved the dry season in Cambodia when the kapok tree pods would ripen, turning from bright green to brown and growing to the size of corn husks. He remembers the large piles of harvested brown pods at his father's trading business in Kampong Thom, where workers removed the white cotton fibres from these pods. To him, the tree was like magic, its fluffy cotton the material of all the pillows and cushions that lined his household. The kapok tree grew everywhere, belonged to no one, and provided for everyone.

In Khmer, the word *kor* means both *kapok* and *mute*. It is said that when the wind blows in Cambodia, the leaves of *doeum-kor*, the kapok tree, make no sound; therefore, the kapok tree is like a person who is mute, or, rather, a person who is mute is like the ancient kapok tree.

During Pol Pot time, Cambodian people recited the proverb *to plant a kapok tree (dam-doeum-kor)* to each other as words of wisdom about how to survive the genocide. To plant a kapok tree, then, exists as a way of knowing, being, and surviving.

[pods]

The kapok tree is a source of livelihood for Cambodian people: its silky fibres are used for textile production and cushion stuffing; its plants and seed pods are eaten as snacks; and its bark can be used medicinally to treat illnesses.

The *Floral Hole* ink drawing by Visoth Kakvei draws us into a space of paradox that confounds and unsettles so much of what we know or think we know about trauma, loss, and survival. When we enter into that space, we delve into a spiral of infinite darkness, but we also swirl into a field of life: a lifeworld, a meditative, repetitious space of beauty, creativity, and regeneration.

The aftermaths of war and displacement are a lifelong process of finding the shape of living and healing. Knowledge of sources of living, and the means to stay silent, makes life in blocked passages habitable, viable, and sometimes even beautiful.

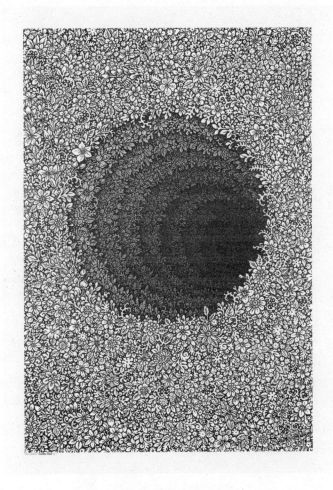

Floral Hole, *drawn by hand with black ink pen (2017).*
Artwork by Visothkakvei. Courtesy of the artist.

Kapok *(2021), sculpture by Sopheap Pich in the shape of a kapok tree pod, made with bamboo, metal, rattan, and a salvaged canoe. Courtesy of the artist.*

[abundance]

One day, when my father is away on assignment with a men's work brigade, he comes across a field of kapok trees.

He knows that the Khmer Rouge regime has now forbidden Cambodian people to forage for food or to plant vegetables of their own. All the resources of the land that provided for Cambodian people for centuries—the trees, the water, the plants—are now the sole property of the state. People are given only two bowls of rice gruel each day. "Stealing" food is punishable by death. And so, many people starve, and watch their loved ones starve, even as the natural abundance of the land flourishes all around them.

On this day, in front of the kapok tree, my father weighs the risks and benefits of defying the regime to feed himself and his family, as he will do hundreds of times over the course of the next four years. This time, he takes the risk. He picks a few pods from the tree, cracks them open, and savours their black, delicious seeds under the cool shade of the tree's quiet branches. For this brief moment, the kapok tree quells his hunger and reminds him of the old days, the happy times, before the war.

[speak]

Sometimes, like the silent branches of the kapok tree, life makes no sound. At other times, life finds a way of speaking through silence, speechlessness, and laboured speaking.

In my family's stories I have searched for ways to listen to and read this difficult ground, to hear its accounts of worlds destroyed and remade. My search has led to my own silence, my own yearning not to see myself—my refugee image—but only to hear myself speak. Why is it so hard for me to speak?

I have yet to meet a Cambodian survivor from my mother and father's generation who is not familiar with the proverb of the kapok tree. Perhaps it is one of the darkest ironies of the Cambodian genocide that those who *did* survive had to learn to tell their story, and to do so often, for whoever wanted to know. Perhaps that is why we have had to become, to some extent, *like the kapok tree.*

It was called "Planting a Kapok Tree" in Cambodia . . . It was more than just keeping one's mouth shut, seeing and hearing nothing; it also meant "don't stand out." Avoid the Khmer Rouge soldiers as interaction breeds emotion and gets one noticed, taken away and never seen again. This logic was used to survive in Pol Pot's new world, his return to year zero, where everything, including emotion and feeling, was extinguished as wrong.

—Karl Levy, *Sinarth: A Dedication to Life*

[pronounce]

February 2020. I give a copy of Souvankham Thammavongsa's recently published short story collection, *How to Pronounce Knife*, to my cousin, whose surname was once Phannavong. She immediately recognizes the author Souvankham's name. *Oh that's definitely a Lao name*, she says.

My cousin Mary has travelled far and wide with me. Countless times we ran through airports after nights of too much drinking and dancing. A tall, long-haired woman with dark skin, she has always been able to smooth-talk her way through airport security; in Paris, Hong Kong, Phnom Penh. In Kuala Lumpur, I was with her when they stopped an entire airplane from taking off so that she could come aboard.

As a child of refugees, my cousin sees something in Souvankham Thammavongsa's name instantly. The way it dances on our tongues with a singsong melody that reminds us of many of the sounds, cadences, and rhythms of Southeast Asia.

I tell my cousin to start by reading the story "You Are So Embarrassing." I believe she will recognize something heartbreakingly true in this story: a resonance with the memories of how our mothers and sisters and aunts had worked on the farm grounds and the factory lines, year after year, as refugees in Canada; I hope she will feel the tinges of excited familiarity, as I do while reading Thammavongsa's stories, at all the references to the joys and sorrows of rural, small-town Canadian life.

My cousin begins to tear up, a drip goes right onto the book's cover. This gift comes at a hard time. My cousin is about to leave Vancouver, the city where we have reunited over the past three years, perhaps forever. I have stopped travelling the globe; she has not.

My cousin remarks that *How to Pronounce Knife* is the first book I have ever given to her by an author with a Lao name. We say my cousin's name aloud, Phannavong, noting how we take on different pronunciations. We say Thammavongsa, laughing and correcting each other, though neither of us is totally certain. We speak together the cadences of the many Lao names that rang throughout our childhoods: Sayavong, Chanthavong, Phromprasack, Rasavong, Vongxay, Khampaseuth.

That's how I was taught to say it!

I'm saying it the way uncle says it!

But the family prefers the anglicized way of saying it!

You're saying it as if it's a Khmer name!

We speak the names again and again. These, the names that filled the wedding halls with seven hundred guests or more at a time. These, the names that created the ingenious worm-picking networks enabling Cambodian, Vietnamese, and Laotian refugees to survive in those early years of resettlement. These, the names that packed a suburban home with dozens of extended family members for a ritual gathering such as a birthday party or a Lao

Buddhist funeral. These names exert a mental and affective pull for us, a nostalgia for an intimate way of being and relating to family, to community, and to the earth and the land.

Names are indelible markers of our histories. When we are asked to change our names, we are being asked to erase our histories. But names are more than this, too—they move across our relations. The difficulties in pronouncing our names can create intimate moments, can move casual encounters to sudden struggles to listen and understand each other. Our names are offerings for these intimacies. When a stranger finds our names too difficult or unintelligible to even try to pronounce, we have learned all we need to know about them.

I have worn many different names throughout my life, sometimes changing my name out of embarrassment and exhaustion, sometimes out of fun and playfulness. In the end, I have always returned to the name that my parents gave me, the gift that tethers me to their past.

I sit with my cousin one last time on our living room couch, a place where we have enjoyed many drinks and shared many stories. We will no longer be around to nourish each other. She is going to a country where she knows no one, where she has no roots. But she holds tight to the book, as if it is not something to be read, but a childhood toy to be cherished. That name on the cover will help carry and transport her, as will the many names that connect us.

Troeung. Tsoi. Y-Dang. Phannavong.

Dearest Kai,

I do not know at what point of your life this letter will find you. Perhaps you are graduating college, perhaps you are getting married, or having a child of your own. As an ill mother, I have no expectation or judgement for you. I hope you will come to these letters to give you life, not restrict it.

When I received my diagnosis, I was in the middle of teaching a class on refugee speculative fiction. In my long-term and slow-building ambition, I imagined that this class would help motivate me to write a book that speculates upon the future for the rest of us. It seems now that this book will never be written, but I find some joy in wondering what your world, two decades from now, will be like.

Since the day I was born, the world has been telling us a story of the refugee. War in my lifetime has been unceasing, and with it the reappearance of peoples who are mistaken as collateral damage. I wonder if war will be as common in your present, or if the world will have settled upon some way to believe, and to believe in, the refugee.

You are likely at a point in your life when you can look back and take some accounting of who you are, and all the things that made you. It has taken me a lifetime to find the right language for telling the stories I have been unable to face. Still, I have refused every impulse to relinquish myself. You too have a story. And like mine, it will always be fertile ground when the languages of the world prove to be unyielding.

I believe in the risk of going there—of dwelling in the space of lived memory and stories. But it is always a struggle. I don't know if you have inherited it: the cycles of fury, depression, self-doubt, mad inspiration, depression, and inspiration again. The tireless labour we do in the hopes and fear of getting it right, only realizing in hindsight that this goal is impossible.

Know that there is no demand, no pressure, to speak or not to speak. To not speak does not mean you have some kind of debilitating silence, or that you are shattered within. It is possible to speak through silence, to use the pieces of our fragmented past to make new worlds.

I don't know how you will remember me at this point in your life. Your father likes to say that I will one day see the impact of my work, but I will be inhabiting the soul of a different body. Perhaps I will be a child in your present. Perhaps my new self will pick up one of my books and some part of me, deep inside, will understand that I am not alone.

If I could reach through time and assure you of one thing, it is the same lesson. You are not alone. Even if I am not with you, you have my writings, you have my letters, my pictures, and my memories. I am always part of you, as you have always been part of me. Even before you were born, we were never an *I*, always a *we*. That is what it means to be beloved, to be family. Just as I once carried you in my womb, you carry me into a future I can only begin to imagine.

love always,
your mom

[landbridge]

The word *sanction* once gave honour, permission, authority. But when Cambodian people were given a sanction, it only imposed a cruel penalty on its people.

Like many countries today that disintegrate under the weight of disease and starvation, Cambodia in the 1980s was relinquished to a devastating famine. During Pol Pot time, Cambodian people like my family lived off two bowls of watery rice gruel a day for almost four years, stunting their capacity for resistance. After the Vietnamese army (America's greatest enemy during this era) invaded Cambodia and deposed the Khmer Rouge in 1979, the West imposed a sanction on foreign aid to Cambodia. No food arrived in Cambodia. No medicine. Nothing.

We didn't have enough of anything, my mother once told me about this time of total insufficiency. The sanctions of war propelled a spiralling exodus of refugees. Some wanted to leave Cambodia forever; others just walked toward the borders in search of food that could not reach the interior.

What emerged from sanctions was the Cambodian land bridge—a human flow of Cambodian people over land from the

The Cambodian land bridge: Cambodian women carry bags of rice from the border camps back to Cambodia. Courtesy of the artist, Ulrike Zöllner.

northwestern regions of Cambodia to the refugee camps at the Thai border. The term *land bridge* comes from the field of bio-geography, and refers to a strip of land that forms across an expanse of water, linking two previously unconnected land masses. The formation of a land bridge allows for a new circuit of migration to take shape.

From 1979 to 1980, Cambodian men, women, and children walked for days to pick up rice, seeds, and tools that had been stockpiled at the border camps. They carried heavy bags of rations on their heads, traversing dangerous paths of landmines, warring militias, checkpoints, dehydration, and the hazards of the jungle. How many women, like my mother, were carrying food on their backs and new life in their wombs as they walked?

In the image of the land bridge, the ingenuity of refugee survival is laid bare alongside the scourge of permanent war. Backward from Cambodia to Laos, Vietnam, and Korea, and forward to Afghanistan, Syria, and Yemen—how far can this bridge wind on?

[wave]

One of the most common injuries suffered by people in war zones is called a concussive wave. When a bomb hits the earth, it sends a shock wave through the air that radiates outward. The effects of these waves on the body and mind are not well studied, but doctors speak of *blast-associated traumatic brain injuries*. Blast traumas, tear connections, shock waves. This is the vocabulary of invisible wounding.

In 1974, concussive waves rippled across Cambodia's capital city of Phnom Penh during a deadly battle at the end of the dry season. With fury in their hearts after years of living under aerial bombardments, the Khmer Rouge guerrillas blasted the city using American 105-mm Howitzers, guns they had acquired on the black market. In retaliation, the US-backed Lon Nol army fought back with their American-made T-28 bomber jets. In the wake of the fighting, the fires came. They blazed through every street, every school, and every home in the city's northeastern residential district, not far from where my parents and two young brothers lived.

I think of Phnom Penh today, in 2021, as another era of war is being called to an end. In 2001, Afghanistan became a new battleground of conflict that burned under the fires of "Operation Enduring Freedom," an occupation that continued for twenty years, and is said to have now ended. As in Cambodia, the war in Afghanistan has left a legacy of invisible wounds and unspeakable grief: one of the largest amputee populations in the world, a collapsed infrastructure, an ongoing refugee exodus.

From 1863 to 1953, Cambodia was a colony of France. War came in 1946, and besides some brief moments of stillness, war did not end until the early 1990s, when the Vietnamese armies finally left the country. By then, war had been present for over forty years. In Afghanistan, too, war has been unceasing, besides a moment of stillness here and there, since 1978, over forty years. Forty years of wave upon wave of bombs and battles and death. Entire generations, submerged.

The long wars wear down a population, slowly, like water corroding a cracked surface. The long wars engulf the lives of soldiers who return home in states of depression, memory loss, PTSD, and shell shock. But these soldiers only spend months, or perhaps a few years, in these waves, and they are always far from home. What can we say about the brain health of people whose sense of war is one of permanence, whose home is war itself?

[broken seed]

In Cambodia, my parents called bombs *kro bike*, which literally meant *broken seed*.

Bombs break nature apart. They pound and pummel the earth far outside the natural cycles of life. Ending lives and maiming bodies, bombs are the antithesis to what the seed embodies—life, growth, and regeneration. Bombs crater and deform the land. They bend and truncate trees. They make the water, air, and homes of human and non-human life uninhabitable for generations to come.

From 1970 to 1973, Cambodia, once known as an *Island of Peace*, wanted no part in the Vietnam War. But the bombs kept arriving, all 2.7 million tons of them, dropped by US airplanes. These broken seeds transformed Cambodia's lush, tropical landscape into a scarred surface, freckled with hollowed-out spots.

Not all the bombs would detonate right away. Some would lay dormant for years, some for decades, just beneath the earth's skin. They would begin to fragment, one by one, triggered by feet foraging for food, or small hands searching for toys.

Today, fifty years later, broken seeds still sprout from the ground. They add to the ticker of body counts and maimings. In the watery craters that Cambodian people today call "bomb ponds," fragile little ecosystems grow.

[land]

A photograph of a scorched landscape outside Phnom Penh captures the early destruction wrought by US bombs. With its monochrome palette of a lone survivor, ruined landscape, and darkened skies, the photo evokes the tones and composition of an apocalyptic death-world.

These reflections call attention to the sonic violence of concussive waves and its tormenting effect. The waves would create madness out of anger, desolation, and despair, which would harden into a militarized collectivity of rebellion that would relentlessly seek its revenge on the *imperialists and landowners* in the years to come.

Madness is featured in the photo's landscape, a surreal and awe-inspiring combination of beauty and terror. The broken seeds create broken infertility. The lone person walking through it does not stand tall against a scarred and sublime landscape, but is, as are all refugees, conjoined with it.

A Cambodian landscape in the aftermath of a US bombing near Takhmao, 1973.
Photo by Colin Grafton. This photo was exhibited as a part of the 2015 exhibition
Phnom Penh Before the Fall, *held at the Bophana Audiovisual Resource*
Center in Phnom Penh. Courtesy of the photographer.

[un done]

Am I nearing the end? I can't help but imagine it, the thing we're all waiting for. The symptoms of death that have not yet emerged.

We are waiting for the day when I will wake up to the jaundice of my skin. I will go into the bathroom and see that my eyes have changed their colour and I will know the day has come.

I am waiting for the day I have blood in my stool, or the day I will have an unexplained fever. We will rush to the emergency room. We will tell the people there I have cancer and I have the signs of end of life, and they will move quickly because they are trained to move quickly when someone is about to die, no matter who they are, no matter how ready for death the person may feel.

The ER physicians will do another scan, give me blood tests, until we're no longer talking to radiologists but to palliative care doctors who will share stories of what it's like to die of this cancer and will ask if I'm ready to discuss the option of dying with dignity.

I am dreading this day like an oncoming meteor. I dread it not just because it is my own death, but because it will be the death of my family's world as it currently stands. They will have to change everything after this day, and so they do everything they can to keep this day from coming.

Every morning that this day has not come, I feel that we've cheated, stolen more time. Some days, I am waiting for the day that I am tired of waiting for the day. On those days, I ask: please, please, one more day.

[debt]

The atrocities that have rippled across Cambodia to our shores evade calculation. We speak of the deaths as countless, the violence as inconceivable, the event itself as outside of our beliefs in reality, in mankind.

Yet as I write this in 2021, the US is still demanding that the debt from the early 1970s—money spent on war munitions and to keep alive the army fighting the Khmer Rouge—must be repaid. It was $278 million in the 1970s; today the debt to the US stands at more than US$700 million.

In February 2017, US Ambassador to Cambodia William Heidt insisted at a press conference in Phnom Penh that "it's in Cambodia's interest not to look at the past, but to look at how to solve this [debt] because it's important to Cambodia's future."

What does it mean to be asked to pay this debt? How do we understand our own pain caused by US bombs as incalculable, yet the deaths caused by those bombs as payable debts?

The US bombing of Cambodia devastated the country's civilian and agricultural infrastructure and contributed to a massive food shortage that paved the way for the United States to step in with a loan to Cambodia in the form of agricultural commodities. The loan was made to the Lon Nol government, a regime seen by many as coming to power illegitimately through a US-backed coup in 1970.

The lender rarely needs the money they lent. What they need is the debt to be permanent, to be, in many senses of the word, *outstanding*—to stand out so much that it covers up any question of reparations, of covert intervention and secret war. Debt masks culpability.

Many Cambodians view debt not as an evasive tool, but as a moral obligation to each other. Our debt means we must redress the harms of the past. Debt connects us to the US, who bombed us, because our shared moral debt creates a relation, a future of working together, a means of healing and repair (thus the word *reparations*).

On Qingming, the annual festival to honour the dead, Cambodian streets fill with small fires that burn fake money or gold in remembrance of our ancestors, transferring commodities that are of the most value to the afterlife. Today, the Cambodian ·riel remains devalued as a national currency. Instead, piles of fake US dollars are set alight.

From the Bomb Ponds *series, 2009, by Vandy Rattana.*
Courtesy of the photographer.

[scape]

Idyllic and tranquil, Vandy Rattana's *Bomb Ponds* photo series (2009) shows former bomb craters overgrown with fecund foliage in Cambodia's eastern provinces.

I feel an articulation of collective wounds in Rattana's photos, an illegibility turned deeply material. I feel the threat that lurks just beneath nature's tranquil surface, those grotesque broken seeds, brought here by a crusade of vested interests.

In one photo, the landscape traces human interaction, both in the bomb that created the crevice, and in the agricultural grid of the rice field that grows around it. The bomb pond remakes land, creates the conditions for new growth. This growth is neither tragic nor optimistic. The muddiness of the pond is reflected in the muddy sky, and trees stand far off, like onlookers. I feel the photo's silence, arriving long after concussive waves have rippled out. It is my own loss of speech that comes from telling one's story of war and trauma again and again and again.

Though silent, the ripples never end. They come in the belated arrival of toxicity and early deaths. They travel to far-reaching rural spaces, the offshored, off-the-grid coordinates where they can never be traced back to a particular source. When we dare do the tracing ourselves, denial meets us at every turn.

When our testimonies are repeatedly invalidated, we must turn to the earth itself as evidence. The ponds that resemble war's continual presence.

[patch]

When and where does the crisis of war begin and end?

Decades of war in Cambodia, we are told, belong to the dark history of a dark nation. War, then or now, can never belong to a single place, time, or people. War is a concussive wave whose ripples never end, though they might go silent. War is the broken seeds that re-create the land, and in turn, those who live and travel upon the land, for as long as that land exists. War is the land bridge that connects us to the faraway places, where war is repeatedly sanctioned anew.

As I write this in 2021, broken seeds are being planted all over the world.

I am thinking today of Syria because I am watching news reports that do not come from American or Canadian media. Like Cambodia in the 1970s, Syria is the terrain of a deadly proxy war. Like Cambodia, Syria is being likened to chess pieces in the war games of global superpowers.

To wage *proxy war* is to find an elsewhere, a sacrifice zone for one's battle. It is the small board for the aspirations of the big players, the hot experiments of the war technicians. Yet, in these terrains of hot fighting, "off the map" of the world's radar, people continue to do what they can to survive.

I see survival in a surreal photo of a man collecting vegetables from a garden patch in Aleppo, Syria, in 2014. He looks to be in his thirties, around the same age my father was during the war in Cambodia. He kneels in the middle of a bright-green circular vegetable patch, balancing three round, white gourds in his hands. The everyday tasks that make up the foreground contrast with the backdrop of a city in ruins. Behind the man rises a wall of collapsed concrete homes, destroyed by explosive-packed barrel bombs tossed from hovering helicopters. The flowering garden patch is the result of a barrel bomb hitting a sewage pipe.

*Aleppo, Syria, September 3, 2014: a man collects vegetables from
a patch residents grew at the site where a barrel bomb hit a sewage pipe in
the Baedeen neighbourhood. Photo by Zein al Rifai/AFP via Getty Images.*

Dearest Kai,

I write this knowing it may be the last piece of writing from me that you will ever receive. I am writing this as the last words of a book that will prepare you for the future, that will teach you all the things that I will not be there to teach.

This book has been about atrocity, pain, and change. But it is not the only story I could have told. Year Zero was supposed to cut us off from our past, and in some ways it did. Many of the oral histories and genealogies were lost. I wrote this book because I do not want us to see this history, Year Zero, as our origin story. It is one of many currents that have brought us to the present and make us who we are.

I return to Pol Pot time because I do not want to be stranded there, at the edge of those mass graves. When we fall into that pit, that dark, swirling place in our minds, we grab hold of our stories for dear life. We hope they will transport us elsewhere, back to our arrival and beyond.

Let me tell you about your own arrival, because it is the beginning of a new story. You were born in Hong Kong at one in the morning, during a summer typhoon. We named you Kai Basilio Troeung, in Chinese, 張愷.

We named you Kai for several reasons. It's the Hawaiian name for sea, and because the character 愷 means joyful and cheerful, and because we loved the character Kai from your Auntie Maddie's novel *Do Not Say We Have Nothing*. The name Basilio comes from your father's great-grandfather Basilio Agsalud, who came to Hawai'i from the Philippines, worked on sugar plantations, and fought in World War I.

Mostly, your name Kai comes from my grandfather, Big Kai, who travelled from Guangdong Province in China to Laos and eventually to Cambodia, and then back to Laos. He was around eighteen years old, escaping conscription in the military, when he travelled to Southeast Asia and became a merchant, setting up all kinds of businesses trading lumber, animal products like skins, and kapok fruits. He could sell anything—he hired workers to go into the jungle and just grab anything that stood out, convinced that he could make it of use to someone, or else his own family. His most memorable trait, your grandparents tell me, was his calmness in the face of any distress or calamity.

There is much more to your name, and to your past, than I can tell you, or than this book has been able to provide you. Maybe you will find solace in the Angkor kingdom centuries past, or perhaps you will visit Guangdong or Fujian, where your great-grandparents once lived. Perhaps you will visit your family in Phnom Penh, or in Laos, and stay up all night as I once did, listening to ghosts while your cousins make fun of you. Or perhaps you will find family and history on your father's side, in Hawai'i, in the Philippines, or in the Scottish, English, and French histories of his father.

By now I am speaking to you alongside the ghosts from the past. We do not seek to haunt you, but to lift when you need lifting, to ache when you ache, to love when you love, to offer memories when you are wanting. The people I've described in this book, including myself, experienced great periods of stress, fear, and deprivation that have left imprints, both spiritual and biological, on their bodies and minds, and on those for generations.

The land bridge was created out of the will to survive, but also out of hope and love. It is all the people who support us, who fly in and out of our lives. It is the book that strikes us, resonates with us, bringing with it not rice or medicine, but words and stories that treat us, help us flourish, prepare us for the darkness ahead. Carry these words, share them with others, and love where you come from, because it is who you are. Remember that, as your grandparents once taught me, when we have nothing, when we are fleeing the soldiers and the bombs, when we are cut off from the rest of the world and each other, we still find some way to come together. With only our bodies and our hearts, we build a bridge.

I love you always and always,
your mom

IN MEMORY

In the morning of November 27, 2022, Y-Dang went gently, surrounded by loved ones. A Cambodian monk and his students came to sing and chant for her in the hours before she died. She passed beautifully, just as she lived.

CITATIONS AND CREDITS

TEXT

xi. *Dictionary of Zoology (5 ed.)* by Michael Allaby
(Oxford: Oxford University Press, 2020).

77, 78. "Snow 'looks nice' to Asian refugees" by Anne Penketh,
from the *Montreal Gazette*, December 4, 1980. Republished
with the express permission of the *Montreal Gazette*,
a division of Postmedia Network Inc.

79. *Running on Empty: Canada and the Indochinese Refugees,
1975–1980* by Michael J. Molloy, Peter Duschinsky,
Kurt F. Jensen, and Robert J. Shalka (Montreal:
McGill-Queen's University Press, 2017).

84. *The Promise of Happiness* by Sarah Ahmed
(Durham: Duke University Press, 2010).

85. *Cambodian Refugees in Ontario: Resettlement, Religion,
and Identity* by Janet McLellan (Toronto: University
of Toronto Press, 2009).

142. "Sihanouk finds caviar and Kim Il Sung mix well" by
John F. Burns, from *The New York Times*, June 22, 1985.

145. *Living Hell: Democratic Kampuchea, August 1978*
by Gunnar Bergstrom (Cambodia: Documentation
Center of Cambodia, 2008).

161. "The Stories They Carried" by Andrew Lam, from
My Viet (Honolulu: University of Hawai'i Press, 2011).

182. "Trial of Former Khmer Rouge Leaders in Turmoil" by
Seth Mydans, from *The New York Times*, June 15, 2011.

215. *The Argonauts* by Maggie Nelson (Minneapolis:
Graywolf Press, 2015).

249. "Etymology of deportation," Harper Douglas, Online
Etymology Dictionary, accessed March 23, 2023.
https://www.etymonline.com/word/deportation.

263. *Sinarth: A Dedication to Life* by Karl Levy
(Self-published, 2015).

VISUALS

3, 141, 180, 277. More information on Colin Grafton's works can
be found at: https://colingrafton.wixsite.com/
phnompenh1973/refugee-camps.

32, 76. Images republished with the express permission
of the *Montreal Gazette*, a division of Postmedia
Network Inc.

101 (top). "Canadian Prime Minister Justin Trudeau greets
16-month-old Madeleine Jamkossian in Toronto,
on Friday, Dec. 11, 2015." Used with permission
from The Canadian Press/Nathan Denette.

101 (bottom). "Pierre Elliott Trudeau welcomes Cambodian refugees in 1980" from the CBC Archives. https://www.cbc.ca/news/canada/ottawa/archives-1980-trudeau-cambodian-refugees-1.3354888 @00:13. Used with permission from CBC.

130. *A Shell guide to Cambodia* by Ġ. V. Smith. Pamphlet published by Societe Shell du Cambodge in cooperation with The Ministry of Tourism Phnom-Penh, 1966.

256. "Kapok in Cambodia" by Leanghort Sok on YouTube. https://www.youtube.com/watch?v=OzFJ8kMWGJI&t=4s @2:54.

ACKNOWLEDGEMENTS

Y-Dang Troeung:
With deepest gratitude to all those who have helped me carry the weight of this book for so long. I hold your names in my heart, always. អរគុណប្រើន.

Thank you to Christopher Patterson, my soulmate and lifeline, without whom this book would never have been published, and to Madeleine Thien, my found sister, who helped usher it into the world.

Christopher Patterson:
Thank you to our families and our "bubbles" who arrived in our time of need and made it possible to write and edit this book. Thank you to our editors and publishers, and to the artists and researchers who gave us permissions and dove into the archives on our behalf. Thank you to the many doctors and nurses who did everything they could for us. Thank you to everyone, the silent and the unnamed, all the people who make the land bridge. You saw us through our most difficult days.